D1405996

THE STONED FAMILY ROBINSON

Copyright © 2011 by F+W Media, Inc.
All rights reserved.
This book, or parts thereof, may not be reproduced in any
form without permission from the publisher; exceptions are
made for brief excerpts used in published reviews.

Published by
Adams Media, a division of F+W Media, Inc.
57 Littlefield Street, Avon, MA 02322. U.S.A.
www.adamsmedia.com

ISBN 10: 1-4405-1270-1
ISBN 13: 978-1-4405-1270-4
eISBN 10: 1-4405-2570-6
eISBN 13: 978-1-4405-2570-4

Printed in the United States of America.

10   9   8   7   6   5   4   3   2   1

Library of Congress Cataloging-in-Publication Data
is available from the publisher.

Certain sections of this book deal with activities that would be in vio-
lation of various federal, state, and local laws if actually carried out. We
do not advocate the breaking of any law. The authors, Adams Media,
and F+W Media, Inc. do not accept liability for any injury, loss, legal
consequence, or incidental or consequential damage incurred by reli-
ance on the information or advice provided in this book. The information in this book is for entertainment purposes only.

Many of the designations used by manufacturers and sellers to distinguish their product are claimed as trademarks. Where those designations appear in this book and Adams Media was aware of a trademark
claim, the designations have been printed with initial capital letters.

This book is available at quantity discounts for bulk purchases.
For information, please call 1-800-289-0963.

To everyone who lived in, or frequented Miller Hall,
Tufts University, circa 1994.

ACKNOWLEDGMENTS

I'd like to thank Wendy Simard and Andrea Norville and everyone at Adams with a giant pipe-full of gratitude for thinking I might be the right choice for this project. I also want to toast Molly Lyons, my agent and friend, for rolling her eyes behind my back where I could pretend she wasn't rolling them over the projects I keep asking her to represent. I love you and everyone at Joelle Delbourgo Associates with my whole heart.

I want to thank my sister, Hilary, for being such a good girl that our parents almost always believed it was "incense" or "I don't know what you're talking about." I have to thank my mom for the previous statement, my grandmother for choosing to love me anyway, and one particular ex-boyfriend for being such a total burnout that it forced me to turn from pot to alcohol. I want to thank my love Aaron for the excellent information about napping in the Reno library and for being so funny and supportive and for letting our dog hump him for several seconds before swatting her off—because it's hilarious. Which leads me to my thank you to the dog.

Finally, I'd like to thank Johann David Wyss for writing his sons such a long-winded diatribe on how to survive in the wilderness, even if most of it turned out to be factually inaccurate—for example, pineapples, turns out, do not grow on trees. Still, it made for a fantastic group of stoners and several cool rides at Disneyworld. I hope you are hanging with my dad in the arms of Jah smoking a fatty and singing something with a very melodic bridge—or just pounding out the rhythm on some heavenly bongos.

CONTENTS

CHAPTER 1

Trying to Get High While Getting Shipwrecked

"Dude, where's our island?"

F or many days we had been tempest-tossed—and our stash was soaked. Six times had the darkness closed over a gnarly scene, and returning light often brought a renewed jones. Meanwhile, the storm raged on and after seven days all hope was lost for finding that magical island to grow our free-range weed unnoticed by narcs.

We were driven completely off course, with no idea as to our whereabouts.

"Dude, where's our island?"

The sober crew had lost faith and were utterly exhausted. The riven masts had gone overboard, leaks had sprung in every direction, and the water, which rushed in like a gravity bong in a frat-house bathtub, gained on us rapidly. But there would be no sweet smoky relief.

Instead of reckless oaths, the seamen now served up desperate cries to Jah to quit harshin' their mellow, mingled with strange and often ludicrous promises to smoke less should deliverance be granted. Every pothead on board commended his soul to the mighty Rastafari, and—taxing already meager brain cells (without the help of salty snacks)—sought a way to survive.

My heart sank as I looked at my family in the midst of these horrors. Our four stoner sons were overpowered by paranoia. "Dear boys," I said, "if the Queen of Sheba will, She can save us even from this peril; if not, let us enjoy one last toke off the emergency joint I kept dry in this precious plastic bag, and think of finding ourselves forever united in that happy half-baked home above. Even dank is not too bitter, if we all pass the Dutchie together."

At these words my weeping wife looked up bravely, and, as the boys clustered round her, she proclaimed, "Let us thank Jah for the dry joint!" She then turned to our teenage and twenty-something sons and held the lit doobie to each of their puckered mouths. I was buoyed by her fortitude, but I was a little annoyed that they were seriously bogarting the J. Fritz, in particular, took a long, hard toke that burned up most of the remaining Mary Jane.

We knelt down together to block the wind. Our spirits were soothed by the comfort of a happy little buzz, and the horrors of our situation seemed less overwhelming. "Ah," I thought. "Jah will hear our prayer! He will help us get together and feel alright."

I was broken out of my excellent haze by a cry of "Land! Land!" but the next instant the ship struck with a frightful shock, causing me to toss the grefa, and totally blow my high. As if that wasn't bad enough, dreadful sounds betokened the breaking up of the ship, and the roaring waters poured in on all sides like a cracked hookah.

Then the voice of the captain was heard above the tumult, repeating as if in a daze, "Shut *UP!*" followed by, "*NUH*-uh!"

I fumbled for the joint, ran up to the deck, and handed the captain the rest of the roach. Seeing how freaked out he was, I composed myself and called out cheerfully, "Take a little pull, my friend! We are all above water. There is land close by where we can dry out our stash and plant more, so let us do our best to reach it. You know Jah helps those who help themselves!"

A wave instantly threw me down, followed by another, and then another, as I tried to find the boxes of doobage we had tied together to hold us over on the voyage. The boxes, when I found them, were shattered on all sides, and one had a large hole in it.

Meanwhile, forgetting the passengers (who were comprised of *me and my family!*), the crew—including that selfish captain—crowded into the lifeboats and cut the ropes to cast each boat into the sea. To my horror, through the foam and spray, I saw the last remaining boat leave the ship with nearly *all of our bud*, regardless of my cries and entreaties that we might be allowed at least a little of the bammy, if not secure a seat on the boat itself. But my voice was scratchy from the harsh joint, and even had the crew wished it, their return was impossible, for the waves were mountain-high.

Casting my eyes despairingly around, I became gradually aware that our position was by no means hopeless, as there remained a single untouched carton still moored to the mast beam of the boat. As the clouds of mist and rain drove past, I could still make out a few fully ripened stems peeking out of the cracks, which I took as a sign of help from Jah in our hour of need.

Yet the sense of our forsaken condition weighed heavily upon me—what with a fully jacked-up ship and nothing dry enough to smoke! As I returned to my family with the soggy carton tucked under my arm, I forced a smile and broke the bad news. "I guess chillin' fireside is out of the question for now. But on the bright side, dear ones, our good ship is so placed that our cabin will remain above water, and

4

tomorrow, if the wind and waves abate, I see no reason why we should not be able to get ashore."

These few words—coupled with the sweet smell from the box of herbal refreshment I had with me—had an immediate effect on the spirits of my children, for my family trusted in my assurances and the smell of weed, wet or dry. The boys at once regarded our chance of escaping as a happy certainty and began to enjoy the miniature buzz-on our little joint had provided.

My wife, however, had a harder time mellowing out. She could tell I was anxious that the crew had stolen most of the weed and that we were going to have to budget scrupulously until a new stash grew—scruples not being our strong suit. I made her comprehend our real situation (using ESP as I always do when we talk in front of the kids). I reminded her that her courage would keep us from a total wig out.

"We must find some food, and have a proper supper," said my good wife, sensing the munchies in us all. "It will never do to grow faint from hunger. We shall require our utmost strength tomorrow."

CHAPTER 2

Finding the Stash

*"When you see how fat a spliff
I will roll you, you will think you are
baby Ziggy climbing onto your
father Marley's cozy lap."*

The day wore on with the storm as fierce as ever, and at intervals we were startled by crashes further damaging our unfortunate ship. We thought of the lifeboats, and feared that they must have sunk under the foaming waves—even though the thieving crew deserved it for stealing the funk, my family did not wish them *dead*.

"Jah will help us soon now, won't He, Father?" asked Franz, the youngest.

"WTF?" said Fritz, my eldest son, sharply, "I finally have a good mellow and this one knocks me out of it with his 'Won't Jah save us, Daddy?'"

"Come on, Fritz, my boy. You too often speak harshly to your brothers but the boy is cold, wet, and about to go through mad withdrawal, so tone it down."

A good meal of Hot Pockets that we had to eat cold (but that we ate cold even when we were not shipwrecked) was finally ready. My sons ate heartily and speedily fell fast asleep. Fritz, who understood the real implication of not having anything to smoke come morning, bugged us all night. After a long excellent silence: "Father," he asked, "can't we try to dry some of this out? I mean, get the boys to sleep on it or blow on it?"

"Your idea is so good that I shall arrange something at once, so that perhaps we can wake-and-bake after all," I responded.

We immediately wrapped the leaves in anything we could find that wasn't drenched, woke my wife and other sons, and instructed them to sleep on top of their new marijuana mattresses. Meanwhile, Fritz and I ran around trying to find important items we might be able to take with us. On the off chance we'd be able to get extra fucked up in the morning, as we were hoping, we'd be certain to forget basics like matches and papers.

Afterward, Fritz drifted to sleep, while throughout the night I searched the boat for any abandoned reefer.

At length the faint dawn of day appeared, the long weary night was over, and with thankful hearts, we found that Fritz had managed to get a few of the marijuana leaves, if not totally dry, basically smokable. Blue sky was seen above us, and the lovely hues of sunrise adorned the eastern horizon.

We assembled on the remaining portion of the deck to toke it up, but my family started complaining about the modicum of dried bomba we managed to get burning.

"Fritz farted on it!"

"I did not!"

"That's how you got it so dry?"

"I have an unusually high body temperature!"

"I'm not smoking that ditch weed!"

"My boys," I interjected, "we have to smoke what we have. Although Fritz does have a high propensity for gas, he also has a freakishly high body temperature. I say that we trust in Jah that He has not forsaken us. And let us pass this thinly packed bowl and be grateful that we even have that!"

"I swear I didn't fart on it," said Fritz.

"Whatever," exclaimed Jack, "I cannot wait to get on shore so I can just chill for half a second without the melodious sounds of your persistent ass-flute."

"That's enough, Jack. Now it's time that I told you all. We have only this one carton of cannabis left. We have to make sure we make it last until we get to shore and can plant another stash."

My wife and sons looked upon our meager stash with no degree of trepidation. For having already left our home, we were unprepared to lose everything we'd brought with us and start again fresh. As stoners, that was going to be *way* too much work.

Unable to smoke that which was already skinned up, we went instead about the boat to see what supplies we could find. I, myself, proceeded to examine, as it was of greatest consequence, the supplies of fresh water within our reach because I had major cotton mouth.

My wife took her youngest son, Franz, who I think is also my youngest son—I'm not 100 percent sure because I still have five days seventeen years ago that are unaccounted for—to attend to the unfortunate animals on board that had been neglected for several days.

Fritz made his way to the arms chest, for he had proven himself capable with a semiautomatic back in our old life. Ernest looked for women's clothing, and Jack went for the captain's cabin, the door of which he no sooner opened, when he discovered a totally hidden stash, plus an entire case of the best seeds we could have hoped for, including Black Gold, not to mention an opened carton of single-wrapped Phillies Blunts. The two large dogs guarding it seemed playful enough—unlike the pits and rotties we were used to bumping into when we'd heisted stashes in the past.

Jack was so happy with his find that he didn't have time to feel fear, anger, or paranoia, and the dogs showed their excitement by licking the boy's face and hands. Seizing the larger by the ears, Jack jumped on his back and, to my great amusement, coolly rode to meet me as I came up the hatchway. I heard the large dog muttering under its breath, "I'm gonna get you, Robinson."

At first, I could not refrain from laughing my head off; then when I saw the dog was not kidding, my laughter abated immediately. It did help me regain my composure, and when we reassembled in the cabin, we all displayed our treasures.

Fritz brought a couple of guns, shot belt, powder-flasks, plenty of bullets, and a bong with a skull and two Skate or Die stickers.

Franz produced a cap full of nails, a pair of large scissors, two books of Snoop Dog cigar papers, an axe, and a nice set of bongos, as well as *two full boxes* of unopened Hot Pockets.

Even Ernest managed to bring about—along with a nice pair of women's underpants—a box of no small size, and he eagerly began to show us the sharp little hooks it contained. His brothers smiled scornfully because they figured he had smoked away enough brain cells to think this might actually be something useful.

"Well done, Ernest!" I cried. "These roach clips, which you have found, may contribute more than anything else in the ship to save our lives by holding on to that last burning ember of goodness before it turns to smoke. But Fritz and Franz, you have also chosen well."

"Will you praise me, too?" said my wife. "I have nothing to show, but I can give you good news. Some useful animals are still alive: a donkey; two goats; six sheep; a purple, red, and yellow dancing bear singing "Uncle John's Band"; a ram; and a cow and a fine pig both big with young. I was just in time to save their lives by taking food to them."

"All these things are excellent indeed," I agreed. Locking my eyes with those of the larger of the two dogs who I am pretty sure subtly spit a hunk of Skoal out of the corner of his mouth, I went on, "but my friend Jack here has presented me with a couple of huge hungry useless dogs who will eat more than any of us."

"Oh, Father! They will be of use! They will help us to protect our stash from wild beasts set on chewing it up!"

"No doubt they will, if ever we do get on shore, Jack; but I must say I don't know how we're going to get there . . . unless we ride on the backs of the dogs . . . ." I spaced out momentarily on this childish fantasy.

"Can't we each get into a big tub and float there?" Jack answered, knocking me out of my own stupor with a dreamy look of his own.

"My child, you have hit on a grand idea," I cried. "That is certainly worth trying. Now, Franz, let me have your tools, hammers, nails, saws, augers, and this"—I snatched the lacy garments out of Ernest's clutched fingers, for I planned to have my wife model them later—"and then make haste to collect any tubs you can find!"

We soon found four large casks, made of wood and strongly bound with iron hoops. They were exactly what I wanted, and I succeeded in sawing them across the middle, even if my work was a little shoddy and I did nearly lose a finger. It was a hard labor, and we were happy to stop and refresh ourselves with Fritz's special—now even more dried out than before, having spent the day in his back pocket— enjoyed with a box-o-wine and Cheetos.

My eight tubs stood ranged in a row on the lower deck near the open door of the gangway. I looked at them with great satisfaction, but to my surprise, my wife did not seem to share my pleasure!

"There isn't enough dooby in the whole of Emperor Selassi's Kingdom," she said, "to give me the courage to get into one of those!"

"Do not be too sure of that, dear wife. When you see how fat a spliff I will roll you, you will think you are baby Ziggy climbing onto your father Marley's cozy lap."

The way I put everything together to make floating tubs for my family was neither efficient nor particularly safe. Still I had no doubt they would float adequately in calm water—so I used my mental powers to calm it. But when we thought all was ready for the launch, we found, to our dismay, that the whole contraption was all so heavy and because our efforts were, frankly, pretty weak, the tubs would not move an inch.

"I must have a little bump," I cried. "Run and fetch any kind of upper you can find!"

Fritz quickly brought a little bit of something that was either chalk dust, or something more—motivating. In no time, I was able to raise the forepart of our tub-boat using no more than brute strength so that my sons could place a rolling dolly under it.

"How is it, Father," inquired Jack, "that with just a little bit of that white dust up your nose, you alone can lift more than all of us together?"

I explained, as well as I could in a hurry, the principle of an enormous burst of dopamine rushing the brain and destroying all gray matter in its wake; at which point Jack said that he, too, could move the world if he had a bit of nose candy. I agreed to discuss this matter with him further when we made it to land—because I did not like the idea of my boys using this offensive drug, unless, like now, it was an emergency.

So with the help of telekinesis, some rope, and another short trip on the white pony, I got the thing, if not safely launched, launched none-the-less into the water. At first, my family had a big laugh because they thought that it was just going to float away and that all of our hard work was going to have been for nothing. Meanwhile, I flipped out in the kind of coke-rage that turned my face red and raised my voice three octaves. Luckily, a rope got caught around Fritz's leg, which was hilarious because he fell over like an unstable water bong, hurt his tailbone, and had to smoke a whole bowl by himself to shut up about it.

We threw some things into our raft, including the crates of stash and the captain's case of seeds. We were all so delighted that we smoked a somewhat soggy celebratory spliff. It was plain to me at once, however, that we'd all need something more to get us calmly to shore. So I gave everyone some of the brandy from the crew mess so that they were adequately blitzed out of their gourds.

After about twenty tries, the boat finally appeared somewhat steady, so I got in. I almost forgot about the wife and boys, but they had the oars for the voyage so I didn't get far. By now we were all just so totally spent and ready to do some serious damage to another bunch of Hot Pockets that we postponed our journey to the island until the next day.

It was not awesome to have to spend another night in a boat halfway stuck between two rocks. But we sat down to enjoy a comfortable supper of Hot Pockets and some Funyuns we'd dug up in a pantry filled with major snack foods.

We prepared for rest in a much happier frame of mind than we had the preceding day, but I did not forget the possibility of a renewed storm, and therefore made everyone put all the loca in Baggies and sleep on top of them. I persuaded my wife (not without considerable difficulty) to put some of it where the kids would never look, in her bra, as a private stash for just us, which led, deservedly, to a stinging smack across my cheek. I ate a stale pot brownie to dull the pain.

She at last consented to do this and left us for a short time, reappearing with much embarrassment and many blushes in a shirt stuffed up top in such a way that—I can say this even though she's the mother of my kids—she looked hot as hell. I told her so, and the kids just ignored us, until any awkwardness she felt soon began to pass. I got to fully enjoy her once we were alone in our hammock, which we followed with a peaceful sleep to prepare us all for the exertions of the coming day.

CHAPTER 3

Floating High and Magic Weed

"Hey, Fritz!" called Jack. "Why don't you chase some cock to put in the tub?"

We rose up early, for sleep weighs lightly on the hopeful as well as on the snockered. After kneeling together for our morning toke, I said, "Now my beloved ones, with Jah's help we are about to effect our escape. Let the animals enjoy the contact buzz with which we will leave them."

The boys joyfully obeyed me because we'd smoked the Buddha and were just cruising. I selected, from the small quantity of cannabis we'd scraped together, Johnsongrass, Kif, P.R., TJ, and some Love Boat, along with a barrel of potlikker tea, a pack of papers, and a didgeridoo. Even so, the boys had brought so much other paraphernalia that we were obliged to leave some of it for a future trip.

With a hearty prayer for Jah's blessing, we now began to take our seats, each in his or her tub. Just then we all collectively imagined the chickens and roosters still on board as breaded and deep-fried, Kentucky style.

"Why shouldn't the birds come with us!" I exclaimed. "If we find no food for them, they can be food for us! Ten hens and a couple of cocks . . ." I roughly counted.

Caught off guard, my family laughed uproariously. "What did I say?" I asked.

"Hey, Fritz!" called Jack. "Why don't you chase some cock to put in the tub?"

To which Fritz responded with a confident middle finger.

After the fowl were accordingly placed together in one of the tubs and secured with some wire netting over the top, we were happy to see the ducks and geese follow us so willingly; that is, after I sent them a mental message that we were their masters. The pigeons, unheeded, swiftly made for the shore. My wife came at last with a gunnysack of poke as big as a pillow in her arms. "This is my contribution," she said, throwing the bag to Franz, as a cushion for him to sit upon to protect himself as the smallest from being tossed from side to side—or just for smoking at will.

All being ready, we cast off and moved away from the wreck. My good, brave wife sat in the first compartment of the boat. Next to her was Franz, our sweet-tempered, alarmingly affectionate little boy, nearly eighteen years old. Then came Fritz, a handsome, spirited young fellow of twenty-four; the two center tubs contained the valuable goods. Then came our bold, thoughtless Jack, nineteen years old. Next to him twenty-one-year-old Ernest, my second son, who one might describe as totally spaced out and/or chronically dipso-ed. I myself, the paranoid but loving father, stood in the stern, endeavoring to guide the raft with its precious cargo to a safe landing-place using my powers of telekinesis.

The elder boys took up pipes. Everyone had his or her own personal joint and something useful close to him, a lighter in a Baggie, in case of being thrown into the water or otherwise separated from the group.

The tide was flowing, which was a great help to my mental powers. We set off from the wreck and glided into the open sea. All eyes were strained to get a full view of the land. For some time we made no progress, as the boat kept turning round and round, until I hit upon the right way to steer it with my mind, after which we clumsily made for the shore.

We had left the two dogs, Turk and Juno, on the wreck, as both were so large we did not have any idea how to move them, plus Turk—the big guy—had thoroughly freaked me out. But when they saw us deserting them, they gave way to piteous howls and sprang into the sea. I was scared for them, because it was a far swim without any uppers to buoy them. But they followed us and, occasionally resting their forepaws on the outriggers, kept up with us well.

"Turk," I said, "you are going to be my faithful companion and friend."

"Or you will be *mine*," he replied cryptically. I almost fell out of my tub and into the water, but the animal winked at me and, having no choice, I winked back.

Our passage, though tedious, was safe. But the nearer we came to the shore the less inviting it appeared. The barren rocks seemed to threaten us with misery and a total lack of doobage.

Many leaves and plastic bags floated on the water around us. Fritz and I managed to secure the crates of ripened leaves, so as to tow them alongside. With the prospect of a weedless-world before us, it was desirable to lay hold of anything likely to contain provisions.

By-and-by we began to see that between the cliffs, green grass and trees were discernible. Fritz could distinguish many tall palms, and Jack hoped they would prove to be coca plants, and enjoyed the thoughts of refining them for entertainment purposes.

"I am very sorry I never thought of bringing the captain's woola," I said, for I knew how much fun it would have been, given this long, boring and frankly uncomfortable journey.

"Oh, look here, Father!" cried Jack, drawing the little spliff-of-happiness out from his pocket.

After we passed it, I engaged with Turk-the-dog in a long, meaningful conversation about whether the color blue as I saw it was the same blue that everyone else saw, or if when I said blue, it meant red or green in the eyes of another—to which he replied that all the world was in fact black and white, which thoroughly blew my mind. All this had taken my attention from my focused telekinetic boat steering while a strong current was carrying us directly toward the rocks, but I was able to use the Force to guide us toward an opening where a stream flowed into the sea. I could then direct our geese and ducks toward this place as well. I steered after them into the creek.

We found ourselves in a small bay or inlet where the water was perfectly smooth and of moderate depth and definitely swirling in myriad psychedelic whirlpools. The ground sloped gently upward from the low banks to the cliffs, which here bent inland, leaving a small plain on which it was easy for us to land. Everyone sprang gladly out of the boat except little Franz. Lying packed in his tub with smoke coming out of his ears, he had to be lifted out by his mother.

The dogs had scrambled onshore before us; Juno received us with loud barking and Turk whispered to me, "Here you will serve me in the kingdom you will build for me to rule." This took me by surprise, given that I thought we had shared such a pleasant and spirited debate on the way over. Meanwhile, the chickens, geese, and ducks kept up an incessant din, added to which was the screaming and croaking of flamingos and penguins, whose dominion we were invading. The noise was deafening, but far from unwelcome to me, as I pictured all of these living birds on plates surrounded by beans and well-buttered bread.

As soon as we could gather our children around us on dry land, we knelt to offer thanks and praise to Jah for our merciful escape, and with full hearts we smoked the crap out of the rest of the pillow that Franz had floated in on, even though Ernest kept saying it was certainly fart-covered.

I then set about finding a suitable place to erect a tent so that I could make some sweet love to my wife. While the boys were jumping off rocks to see if they could fly, my wife and I "erected the tent" thusly: Thrusting my long spar into a hole in her rock, and supporting the other end of my firmly planted pole, she placed her heavy chest close and her box near the border of my canvas, arranging herself so as to allow me to be close to her entrance . . . and so forth.

After the tent was "raised," the boys, having given up on their fun, ran inside to arrange their beds, while I created a fireplace, surrounded by large flat stones near the brook that flowed close by. Dry leaves and Zacatecas Purple were soon ablaze on the hearth. I filled the iron pot with pot-iron tea, and after I gave my wife several pot-cakes, she established herself as our cook, with Franz to help her.

He, thinking his mother was melting some glue for sniffing, wanted to know, "What are we going to make next?"

"This is to be for your dinner, my child. Do you think these pot-cakes look like glue?"

"Yes, indeed I do!" replied Franz. "And I would very much like to sniff glue pot-cake soup! Don't you want some, Mamma?"

"Where can I get glue, dear?" she asked. "We are a long way from any superstore! But these pot-cakes are made of the juice of good leaves, boiled till they become a strong stiff jelly—which will make nice soup."

Fritz, leaving a loaded gun with me, took another himself and went along the rough coast to see what lay beyond the stream. This fatiguing sort of walk would not suit the average stoner's fancy, so Jack sauntered down to the beach, and Ernest scrambled among the rocks searching for paisley patterns and talking sea turtles.

I was anxious to land the two casks of Everclear that were floating alongside our boat, but on attempting to do so, I found that I could not move them telekinetically up the bank on which we had landed and was therefore obliged to look for a more convenient spot. As I did so, I was startled when I heard Ernest shouting for help, as though in great danger. He was some distance away, and I hurried toward him with a hatchet in my hand.

The little fellow stood screaming in a deep pool, and as I approached, I saw that a huge lobster had caught his nose in its powerful claw—not my brightest child, he was probably trying to kiss it. Poor Ernest was in a terrible fright, and strike as he would, his enemy still clung on. I waded into the water, and seizing the lobster firmly by the back, managed to make it loosen its hold, and we brought it safely to land.

Ernest, having taken a quick shlook off the lit J I was holding, speedily recovered his spirits, and anxious to take such a prize to his mother, caught the lobster in both hands. He instantly received such a severe blow from its tail that he flung it down and passionately hit the creature with a large stone calling it, "Murray," and telling it that he was no one's daddy.

This display of temper vexed me. "You are acting in a very childish way, my son," I said. "The lobster, it is true, gave you a bite, but then you, on your part, intend to eat it. So the game is at least equal."

Once more lifting the lobster, Ernest ran triumphantly toward the tent. "Mother, Mother! A classy dinner! None of those white-trash saltines and Spam for us! A lobster, Jack! Look here, Franz! Careful, he'll bite you! Where's Fritz?"

Everyone came crowding around Ernest and his prize. He wanted his mother to make lobster soup directly, by adding it to what she was now boiling.

She, however, begged to decline making any such experiment and said she preferred her pot-soup without any googly-eyed shellfish—as she referred to the poor offending lobster. Something of a connoisseur of lowbrow foods, my wife was known to choose Cheez Whiz and Wonder Bread over Gouda and Triscuits every time. I let them fight about it.

He—"But snop soup and lobster is food fit for a king!"

And she—"I won't eat that foul creature even if it is, as they say, a perfect conduit for pot-butter."

Meanwhile I returned to the beach where I could ride out my blitz in unadulterated bliss.

On my return I resumed the subject of Ernest's lobster— even though they had already moved on to debate whether or not the original *Mad Max* was so exceptional a film that it leant some credibility to its abysmal triquel, *Beyond Thunder Dome*—I told Ernest he could have the lobster all to himself when it was ready to be eaten, finally congratulating him on ultimately remembering that he had caught a lobster today.

"Now," said my wife, tasting the soup with the stick with which she had been stirring it, "it's no Cream of Mushroom soup over Stove Top stuffing, but it will do in a pinch. And where can Fritz be?" she continued, a little anxiously. "And how are we to eat our soup when he does come?" she continued, beginning to sound a little bit like she'd sampled enough pot-soup for one day. "We have no plates or spoons. Why didn't we remember to bring some from the ship?"

"Because, my dear, one cannot think of everything when one is so pleasantly high."

"But we can't lift the boiling pot to our mouths," she argued.

I was forced to agree. We all looked upon the pot with perplexity. Our silence was at last broken, when all of us burst into wild laughter at our own folly in not remembering that spoons and forks were things of absolute necessity.

"Really though, oyster-shells would do," said Jack, after a moment's thought.

"True, that is an idea worth having! Off with you, my boys, get the oysters and clean out a few shells. And none of you must complain because the spoons have no handles, and we burn our fingers a little in bailing the soup out."

When they returned, we heard a shout from Fritz in the distance. We returned it joyfully, and he appeared before us, his hands behind his back, and a look of disappointment upon his face.

"Unsuccessful!" he said.

"Really!" I replied. "Never mind, my boy, better luck next time."

"Oh, Fritz!" exclaimed his brothers who had looked behind him. "An entire branch of Acapulco Gold! Where did you get it? Are we in Acapulco? Do let us see it!"

Fritz then with sparkling eyes exhibited his prize.

"I am glad to see the result of your prowess, my boy," I said, "but I cannot approve of deceit, even as a joke. Stick to the truth in jest and earnest."

"What?" asked Ernest.

"No, I mean, even when you aren't joking, you should stay truthful," I explained, "you know, in jest or in *earnest*."

"I said, 'What?!'" came Ernest's reply.

"No! 'Earnest!' not 'Ernest!' E-A-R . . . oh never mind."

Fritz, rolling his eyes, then told us how he had been to the other side of the stream. "So different from this," he said. "It is really a beautiful country, and the shore, which runs down to the sea in a gentle slope, is covered with acres and acres of fully ripened marijuana plants!" Fritz's eyes sparkled as he bowed his head in reverence. "You will not believe the bounty of it, Father. It is so much that I must say, I will live beside you, my family, in this joyful place, but as a testament to my love and gratitude for my savior, Jah, I will not smoke reefer again, until He deems it should be so."

"Stop, stop, my boy!" I cried, alarmed by what had led my eldest to such a shocking proclamation.

"I prayed to Jah to save our stash," he continued. "But what He has given us is beyond my wildest dreams; therefore, I must pay him back with my avowed abstinence."

"But it's Acapulco Gold!" said Jack.

"It was one of several varietals," said Fritz, "growing in abundance on the island. There are also some very curious little plants that, after I smoked them, made me squat down on my hind legs and rub my snout with my forepaws. Had I been less afraid of losing my mind completely, I would have tried to smoke one more, it seemed so tame. But no more was as easily taken." And we could tell by the crusting at the corners of his mouth that he had tossed some of his morning Hot Pockets during his adventures.

Meanwhile, Jack had been carefully examining the branch in question.

"This is no Acapulco Gold," he said, "and except for its bristly buds, does not look like one. See, its crystals are not like those of a Mexican breed, but rather those of one from Africa. In fact," he continued, looking at Fritz, "your Acapulco Gold is an African Blue."

"Damn," said Fritz, "listen to the great professor lecturing!"

"You need not be so quick to laugh at your brother," I said. "He is quite right. I, too, know the African Blue by descriptions and pictures, and there is little doubt that this is a specimen. The little leaves grow under trees. Its flesh is white but dried, and it never entirely loses a certain wild flavor, which is disagreeable to uptight Frenchmen. It is held in great esteem by the natives, especially when the flora has grown near the sea where it has been impregnated with salt."

"You said, 'impregnated!'" laughed Ernest.

I went on, "But, Jack, the African Blue not only looks something like Acapulco Gold, it most decidedly makes a man grunt like a porker.

"Now," I continued, "who will try this delicacy?" All at first hesitated to partake of it so unattractive did it appear. Fritz, now an avowed straightedge, walked away entirely. Jack, however, tightly closing his eyes and making a face as though about to take medicine, took a long drag from the pipe I had packed. We followed his example, one after the other, discounting my eldest, and thereby provided ourselves with a mind-blowing buzz.

After we had done several line dances, including "Boot Scootin' Boogie" by Brooks and Dunn, and then braided cornrows into Ernest's hair, our soup was ready. Gathering round the pot we dipped in the oyster-shells, not, however, without scalded fingers. Fritz ate the discarded oysters since he knew the soup was laced. Jack meanwhile drew from his pocket a large shell he had procured for his own use while the rest of us just had little ones, and scooping up a good quantity of soup he put it down to cool, smiling at his own foresight.

"Prudence should be exercised for others, not just for oneself," I remarked, confusing everyone, so I restated: "Do you really think you are so much better than your brothers? Your enormous shell of soup will do capitally for the dogs, my boy. Take it to them, and then come and eat like the rest of us."

Jack winced at this, but silently taking up his shell, he placed it on the ground before the hungry dogs, and they lapped up its contents in a moment. He returned, and after waiting for the soup to cool some more, we all ate our dinner merrily.

While we were thus employed, we suddenly discovered that our dogs, not satisfied with their mouthful of soup, had spied the African Blue and were rapidly tearing it apart. The boys all began to yell, and Fritz, fighting for the gift that Jah had bestowed, first threw a stone at the dogs and then, seizing his gun, flew to rescue it from their hungry jaws. Before I could prevent him, he struck Turk with such force that his gun was bent. The poor beast ran off howling, "Let it be known, your boy Fritz will pay for this!" The dog's cry came over his shoulder and was met by a shower of stones from Fritz, who yelled at him so fiercely, that if I had not interfered, it was probable he would have killed them.

"Dude," I scolded, "I know you are up against the wall right now, but you are going to have to *chill!*"

I followed Turk, and as soon as he would listen to me, explained to him how despicable as well as wicked such behavior inarguably was. But I added that the boy was in heavy withdrawal. I could not let it pass, without comment, that "you have threatened my child."

"I will threaten again and you will do as I say" came the savage reply.

I then felt my body forced down to one knee. "Kneel before Zod," said Juno, coming up behind us.

"I thought your name was Turk," I replied, still kneeling.

"Some people call me Zod," explained the dog. "I answer to both."

I was released and sent back to camp. Fritz's temper had always been easily aroused, but it never lasted long when it could be soothed with a deep and cleansing bong hit. However, even without such assistance, he recovered himself and expressed sorrow for his behavior.

"You should probably apologize to the dog," I cautioned, but he just raised his eyebrow and then laughed as though I had said something funny.

"No, really," I repeated, but by then the whole family was howling and rolling on the ground. "To Turk, I mean. You should apologize. He was really mad."

By this time the sun was sinking beneath the horizon, and the poultry, which had been wandering around to quite a distance and back, now gathered around us, and began to pick up the crumbs that had fallen during our meal. My wife then drew from her bag some handfuls of pot-brownie crumbs from the stale brownie stash to feed the poultry—an exceptional idea, which I have to admit, was a bit of a turn-on for me.

She, at the same time, showed me a few packages of Reese's Peanut Butter Cups and two boxes of Little Debbie Swiss Cake Rolls. "That was indeed thoughtful," I praised.

The pigeons now flew up to crevices in the rocks, the fowls perched themselves on our tent pole, and the ducks and geese waddled off to plot with the dogs about a potential overthrow. We, too, were ready for sleep, and having loaded our guns and offered up our prayers to Jah, thanking him for his many mercies and gifts to us by smoking a well-packed bowl, we commended ourselves to his protecting care. As the last ray of light departed, we closed our tent and lay down to rest.

The children remarked on the suddenness of nightfall, that there had been little or no twilight. This convinced me that African Blue must really make the time fly by. "Maybe it's magic weed," I thought, "so when the sun sinks, it produces what seems to be sudden darkness."

"Magic weed . . ." I whispered, smiling, then dreamily pondering the vast resources on this great island, fell soundly asleep.

CHAPTER 4

Not Really Discovering So Much as Stumbling Over the Dank

"But, Father, we're old enough to get sozzled with you and Mother. Why aren't we old enough for this?"

We would have been badly off without our tent, for the night proved as cold as the day had been hot, but we managed to sleep comfortably, everyone being thoroughly fatigued by the many refreshments of the previous day.

The voice of our vigilant cock roused me at daybreak, and when I explained to my family that I awoke at daybreak because "the vigilant cock roused me!" everyone laughed heartily—although I wasn't certain why, until about two hours later when I got it. We all decided that if possible we should find out the fate of our crew and then further examine the nature and resources of the country on which we were stranded.

We therefore came to the resolution that we would eat a breakfast of some cold pot-cakes with a hookah toke, except Fritz. To our mild amusement and a general murmur of "We'll see how long this lasts," he ate some eggs from our hen with oysters. Then Fritz and I started off on our expedition, while my wife remained near our landing-place with the three younger boys.

However, at the mention of an excursion, all four children wanted in on the action.

"Steady there, steady!" I said. "You cannot all come. Such an expedition as this would be too dangerous and fatiguing for you younger ones."

"But, Father, we're old enough to get sozzled with you and Mother. Why aren't we old enough for this?" they asked.

Not having a good answer, I replied simply, "Fritz and I will go alone this time, with one of the dogs"; then I used my powers of telepathy to quell any further dissention. "Fritz, prepare the guns, and tie up Juno so that she will not follow us."

At the word *guns*, the poor boy blushed shamefully. He tried in vain to straighten the weapon with which he had angered the powerful Turk the night before. I left him alone for a short time, hoping he would feel enough remorse to offer his regrets to the dog.

A moment later he tried to lay hold of Juno to tie her up, but the dog, recollecting the blows she had witnessed the night before, began to snarl and would not go near him. Turk began chanting, "Lowly human, you will serve Turk and Juno," and I found it necessary to call out, "We are your loyal subjects, Masters Turk and Juno," to induce them to approach us. Fritz made his peace with the dogs by sharing his oyster omelet, which I could see, pleased at least Juno. However, Turk, who was of a fiercer and more independent temper, still held off, watching him with great distain.

"Give him a claw of this lobster I just found," cried Ernest, forgetting that he had actually caught the lobster the day before and had housed it in a bucket to eat at his own leisure. "Then you can take the rest for your journey."

With that treat, Turk seemed appeased and said to me in a gritty low voice, "You see, Old Man? What Turk wants, Turk gets." Fritz and I then armed ourselves, each taking a gun and a dime-bag—although I knew Fritz did so by force of habit and did not intend to smoke it. Breakfast being over, we stowed away the remainder of the lobster and some buttermilk biscuits, with a flask of bourbon, and were ready for a start.

"Stop!" exclaimed Fritz, "we have left something very important undone."

"Surely not," I disagreed.

"Yes," he said, "we have not yet said our morning prayers. We are only too ready, amid the cares and pleasures of this life, to forget Jah to whom we owe all things." I noticed my wife roll her eyes, which almost made me burst out chuckling at our son's newfound devotion, but we all acquiesced, commending ourselves to Jah's protecting care. I took leave of my wife and children, and asking them not to wander far from the boat and tent (not that it was likely given how much pot had recently come into our possession), we parted with some anxiety on either side, for we had all already smoked a lot of weed that morning.

We now found that the banks of the stream were so rocky on both sides that we could only get down to the water by one narrow passage. I was glad to see this, however, for I now knew that my wife and children were in a comparatively inaccessible spot, the other side of the tent being protected by steep and precipitous cliffs. Any paranoid guy, even one on a deserted island, could only but hope for the same.

Fritz and I pursued our way up the stream until we reached a point where the waters fell from a considerable height in a cascade and where several large rocks lay half covered by the water, which is how we crossed the stream in safety. So with the sea on our left, and a long line of rocky heights, here and there adorned with clumps of trees, stretching inland to the right, we walked on.

We had scarcely forced our way fifty yards through the long rank doradilla grass, which was partly withered by the sun and tangled, when we were alarmed to hear a rustling behind us. When we looked round, we saw the grass waving to and fro, as if some animal were passing through it. Fritz, still going through withdrawal-rage, instantly turned and brought his gun to his shoulder, ready to fire the moment the beast should appear.

I was pleased with my son's coolness and presence of mind, for it showed me that at times having a straightedge companion is a true help in the unknown. This time, however, no savage beast rushed out, but the crazy dog Turk. In my marijuana stupor, I had forgotten to bring him along, and so he had come of his own accord to, in his own words, "watch my every move."

From this little incident, however, we saw how dangerous our position was and how difficult escape would be should any beast come upon us unaware. We therefore made our way to the open seashore. Here the scene that presented itself was indeed delightful. A background of hills, the green, waving grassy fine stuff, pleasant groups of fraho trees stretching here and there to the very water's edge—all formed a lovely prospect.

On the smooth sand we searched carefully for any trace of our hapless ship's crew, but not the mark of a footstep or the roach of a smoked doobie could we find. "Should you fire up a spliff?" Fritz asked. "That would bring them out, if they are within smelling distance."

"It would," I replied, "or any savages who might want some. No, no. Let us search diligently, but as invisibly as possible."

"Okay, Father, but I don't know why we should trouble ourselves about them at all. They left us to fend for ourselves, and I, for one, don't care to set eyes on them again."

"You are wrong, my boy," I said. "In the first place, we should not return evil for evil. Then, again, they might be of great assistance to us in building a house of some sort. And lastly, you must remember that they might not have any fire or pipe in which to spark up within the bounty of this glorious island—and that is a cruelty no stoner should have to bear."

"But, Father, while we are wandering here and losing our time almost without a hope of benefit to them, why shouldn't we return instead to the shipwrecked vessel and save the animals on board?"

I replied, without making eye contact with Turk whom I knew to be studying me closely, "Saving the life of a man is a more exalted action than contributing to the comfort of a few quadrupeds that we have already supplied with food and a fine buzz for at least a few days." When I heard the dog clear his throat, not without an undertone of threat, I added quickly, "Also, the sea is so calm at present that we need not fear that the ship will sink or break up entirely before we can return."

Thus talking, we pushed on until we came to a pleasant grove of exquisite AK-47 bud, which stretched down to the water's edge. Here we stopped to rest, seating ourselves in the shade of a large tree by a small river that murmured and splashed along its pebbly bed into the great ocean before us.

I packed the one-hitter for myself, as Fritz and I gazed around. My son suddenly started up. "A monkey!" he exclaimed. "I am nearly sure I saw a monkey."

"It's probably just your buzz," I reassured him.

He looked at me oddly for a moment and then set off. His excited hallucination amused me so much that when he returned with an object he called "a bird's nest," I was nearing hysterics.

Catching my breath I managed to say, "You need not necessarily conclude that every round hairy thing is a bird's nest, Fritz. There are a lot of round hairy things in this world. I mean, think about all the round hairy things within our trousers alone!" Then coming back to the matter at hand, I added, "This, for instance, is a coconut."

My son blushed as the dog chuckled in amusement at the boy's idiocy. Now that Fritz was sober he'd have fewer excuses for making mistakes like that.

Not without difficulty, we split open the nut, but, to our disgust, found it dry and uneatable.

"Hullo, Nurse!" cried Fritz, "I always thought a coconut was full of delicious sweet liquid, like almond milk."

"So it is," I replied, "when young and fresh, but as it ripens, the milk becomes congealed and in course of time is solidified until it bursts through the shell and, taking root, springs up a new tree." I was pleased to note smoking all that goof butt hadn't erased much of my long-term memory.

It was not without difficulty that Fritz finally found a coconut that was not dried up. It was a little oily and rancid, but this was not the time to be too particular—and after all that I'd smoked that morning, I couldn't really taste it anyway. The milk was refreshing enough to defer additional food until later in the day and so spare our stock of provisions.

Continuing our way through a thicket, which was so densely overgrown with all manner of cannabis growth that we had to clear a passage with our hatchets, we again emerged on the seashore beyond and found an open view of the forest sweeping inland. In the space before us stood single pot plants of remarkable appearance. These at once attracted Fritz's observant eye, and he pointed to them, exclaiming, "See what strange bumps there are on the stems."

We approached to examine them, and I recognized them as rangoon—wild-grown marijuana, the crystals of which grow in this curious way on the stems. "These," I remarked, "are the reason, my boy, you are going to be so sad you gave up the toke."

"Oh, but that is impossible," returned Fritz. "I am quite sure I have done the right thing by Jah and all his prophets, including civil rights leader Marcus Garvey."

"I did not say Jah would be unhappy, Fritz. But *you*, oh wow, you are going to miss out on some fresh shit. When the flowers of these plants have been divided among the rest of us, you are going to regret the promise you made."

"That is a very opinionated notion on your part, Father," said a determined Fritz.

"The friends of Columbus thought it very easy to make an egg stand upon its end when he had shown them how to do it," I cautioned.

But Fritz looked at me blankly so I added, "Now, suppose we cut down some of this beauty to dry out, that it may be ready for use when we take them home."

Fritz instantly took up his knife and tried to cut the stems, but in vain: the blade slipped, and they were cut jaggedly. "What a nuisance!" said Fritz, flinging the knife. "The thing is too hard to cut through; and yet it seemed so simple."

"You are too impatient," I replied. "Those branches are not useless, to those of us who are prepared to ingest THC by way of suppository if that is the only option available." I took from my pocket a piece of string, which I tied tightly around several branches. When this was accomplished, I tied the string yet tighter, and drawing the ends with all my might, the branches fell in two pieces, divided neatly into small clusters as I wished.

"That is clever!" cried Fritz. "What in the world put that plan into your head?"

"Stoners are the most resourceful of all men," I replied. "When it comes to the growing, harvesting, moving, and ingesting of cannabis in any form, we will develop some plan. Be it a pipe carved out of an apple or a dryer sheet over a paper-towel roll to inhibit the smell of the illicit drug when smoked in a college dorm room."

With that, we continued our harvest as the day wore on.

CHAPTER 5

The Monkey on Our Back

"It spooged on me!" he cried in disdain.
"Taste it," I ventured.

After three hours or more, we pushed forward, keeping a sharp lookout on either side for any trace of the desperate crew until we reached a bold ascent from whose rocky summit I knew we should obtain a good and comprehensive view of the surrounding country. With little difficulty we reached the top, but the most careful survey of the beautiful landscape failed to show us the slightest sign or trace of human beings.

"What about those greenhouses over there?" Fritz asked when I commented on the vast untainted island surrounding us.

"What?" I asked, taking a smoke break and closing my eyes.

"I mean, that's man-made, as are those obviously farmed fields down there. Someone had to have been here to plant all of this. . . . And what about those hydroponic farms? Those were impressive."

"Yes, kiddo," I agreed, although as they say, in one ear and out the other. "We are certainly the only human beings who have ever come across this place."

Before us stretched a wide and lovely bay, fringed with yellow sands, either side extending into the distance. The scene inland was no less beautiful, perhaps even more so because of the green and gold stalks of sweet sinsemilla growing there. Yet Fritz announced a feeling of apprehension stealing over him as he gazed on our utter solitude, that although they might be gone now, someone would one day come back for this.

"It would be worth a fortune at any of the Seven Sisters colleges alone. . . ."

"Cheer up, Fritz, my boy," I said, encouragingly. "Remember that you chose your straightedge life. You wouldn't notice any of whatever-it-is-you-are-talking-about if you'd get yourself reacquainted with all the many villages of Mary's and Jane's out there—With Jah's help, let us endeavor to live here contentedly, thankful that we were not instead cast upon some freezing cold habitat without a Snuggie."

Fritz commented on the heat, which once noticed became progressively unbearable. We descended the hill and made for a clump of ganja bushes, which we saw at a little distance. To reach this, we had to pass through a dense thicket of Chronic, which proved a pleasant task for me and a nearly unbearable one for my good son.

Sending Turk in advance, I cut one of the reeds, thinking it would be a more useful weapon than my gun against all the reptilian shapes with which my eyes were tricking me. I had carried it but a little way when I noticed a thick juice exuding from one end. I tasted it and, to my delight, found it sweet and pleasant. I knew at once that I was standing in sugar cane—a great find for any stoner!

Wishing Fritz to make the same discovery, I advised him to cut a cane for his defense. He did so, and as he beat the ground before him, the reed split, and his hand was covered with the juice.

"It spooged on me!" he cried in disdain.

"Taste it," I ventured.

"Gross!" he replied. But with some coaxing, he finally carefully touched the cane with the tip of his tongue; then, finding the juice sweet, he did so again with less hesitation. A moment afterward he sprang back to me, exclaiming, "Oh, Father, that is delicious! We must prepare some of this sugar to bring home to Mother and her never-ending sweet tooth."

"Gently there," I replied, "take a breath for a moment, and remember moderation in all things. We will cut some to take home if you like."

In spite of my warning, my son cut a dozen or more of the largest canes, and stripping them of their leaves, carried them under his arm. We then concluded our cane break and reached the clump of palms for which we had been heading. As we entered it, a troop of monkeys that had been playing on the ground sprang up, chattering and grimacing, and before we could clearly distinguish them, they had sprung up to the very tops of the trees.

Fritz was so provoked by his sudden sugar high that he raised his gun and would have shot one of the poor beasts.

"Wait," I cried, "never take the life of any animal needlessly."

I glanced at Turk who nodded, encouraging me to continue. "A live monkey up in that tree is of more use to us than a dozen dead ones at our feet, as I will show you."

Saying this, I gathered a handful of small stones, and threw them up toward the apes. I heard Turk growling at me, but I persisted. The stones did not go near them, but influenced by their instinctive mania for imitation that I had often seen replicated by my son Ernest, they seized all the coconuts within their reach and sent a perfect hail of them down upon us.

Fritz was delighted with my stratagem, and rushing forward picked up some of the finest of the nuts. We drank the milk they contained, drawing it through the holes we first pierced. The milk of a coconut is excellent for quenching thirst and subduing cotton mouth. We then broke the coconuts because what we liked best was a kind of solid cream that adheres to their shells, which we scraped off with our fingers.

After this delicious meal, we thoroughly despised the rotting lobster we had been carrying all day and threw it to Turk, who ate it insisting that he had forced us to pass it along to him using his powers from Krypton. Meanwhile, I slung a couple of the nuts over my shoulder, fastening them together by their stalks (it wasn't my first time), and, Fritz having finished his prayers, we began our homeward march.

I soon discovered that Fritz found the weight of his canes considerably more than he expected. He shifted them from shoulder to shoulder, then carried them under his arm, and finally stopped short with a sigh. "I had no idea," he said, "that I had become so unbelievably out of shape smoking reefer and playing World of Warcraft all day long while eating Hot Pockets and Honeycomb cereal. I now will add to my vow to my maker, that I will become strong, able, and most of all *useful*. Right, Father?"

I nodded vaguely because I totally hadn't been listening.

"Never mind, my boy," I added, figuring it would go with most grand statements in one way or another. "Patience and courage! Do you not remember the story of Aesop and his breadbasket, how heavy he found it when he started, and how light at the end of his journey? Let us each fasten our bundles crosswise with your gun."

Fritz, thoroughly confused by my instructions, instead began to suck most vigorously on the end of one sugar cane, so that it would have embarrassed me if we had been in public, but he could not extract a drop of the juice.

"How do you get the juice out?" he asked rhetorically.

"Think a little," I replied, "you are the sober one of us—although that might be your problem right there. You do not *want it* as bad as my munchies have made me want it." And I demonstrated by easily withdrawing the delightful juice.

"Of course, I want it," he countered, "but it is like trying to suck marrow from a marrow bone, without making a hole at the other end."

I watched an understanding dawn on my son's sober face. He was going to have to learn how to think in a whole new way under his new oath.

Fritz cut the other end of the sugar cane and speedily perfected the accomplishment of sucking it.

I hastily pulled down the swinging flask from my shoulder. Tugging out the cork, with a loud *pop*, the contents came forth—whiskey flowed freely.

I offered some to my son who drank it happily.

"There, now!" I said laughing, as he tasted this luxury. "You will have to exercise moderation, friend Fritz! I daresay it is delicious, but it will go to your head, if you venture deep into that flask."

"My dear Father, you cannot think how good it is after a whole day of sobriety! I promised Jah I would part ways with the smoke of sweet Mary Jane, but I never swore to give up Jack!"

We were both invigorated by the tipple and went on so merrily after it that the distance to the place where we had left our stems of cannabis seemed less than we expected. We found them quite dry and very light and easy to carry.

Just as we passed through the grove in which we had breakfasted, Turk suddenly darted away from us and sprang furiously among a troop of monkeys, who I could have sworn were doing their taxes on small wooden calculators on the turf at a little distance from the trees—although I had also recently enjoyed a bowl of Afghooie. The animals were taken completely by surprise, and the dog, now ravenous, had seized one and was fiercely tearing it to pieces before we could approach the spot. I knew he would soon be recruiting the others into his army after this unmistakable display of power.

His luckless victim was the mother of a tiny little monkey, which, being on her back when the dog flew at her, had hindered her flight. The little creature attempted to hide among the weed and, in trembling fear, watched the tragic fate of its mother.

On perceiving Turk's bloodthirsty design, Fritz eagerly rushed to the rescue, flinging away all he was carrying and losing his hat in his haste. It was too late for the poor mother ape, but I couldn't help laughing as the young monkey bounded onto the boy's shoulders and held fast to his thick curly hair, firmly keeping its seat in spite of all the shaking Fritz was doing in an attempt to dislodge it. He screamed and plunged about as he endeavored to get the creature off, but it was all in vain, for it only clung closer to his neck.

I laughed so much at this ridiculous scene that I could scarcely assist my terrified boy out of his awkward predicament. Indeed, I told Fritz that the animal, having lost its mother, seemed determined to adopt Fritz. "Perhaps he has discovered in you something of the air of a father of a family."

"But, Father," Fritz moaned, "he is yanking my hair terribly. Can't you get him off?"

At last, by coaxing the monkey, offering it a bit of biscuit, and gradually disentangling its small paws from the curls it grasped so tightly, I managed to relieve poor Fritz, who then looked with interest at the baby ape, no bigger than a kitten, as it lay in my arms.

"What a jolly little fellow it is!" he exclaimed. "Let me have it, Father. I daresay coconut milk will do until we can bring the cow from the shipwreck. If he lives he might be useful to us. I believe monkeys instinctively know what fruits are wholesome and what are poisonous."

"Well," I agreed, "let the little orphan be yours. You will likely need a friend now that you will basically be on your own while the rest of us continue to party."

Turk was meanwhile devouring with great satisfaction the little animal's unfortunate mother. I shuddered. He was clearly demonstrating his great power every chance he had. I saw him glance at me with a smirk. Fritz wished to drive him away from the feast, but I did not want to go to battle with him, not yet, not until I was better prepared, so I suggested to Fritz that he show some gratitude to the dog for giving him a friend of his own. The boy looked at me with a momentary glimmer of worry and then we resumed our march, conversing as we walked.

The tiny ape seated itself in the coolest way imaginable on Fritz's shoulder—like a hot blonde on Fonzi's chopper— and we had gone some distance before Turk overtook us, looking uncommonly well pleased and licking his chops as though recalling the memory of his disgusting feast.

He took no notice of the monkey, but the monkey was very uneasy at the sight of him and scrambled down into Fritz's arms, which was so annoying to the boy that he devised a plan to relieve himself of his burden.

Calling Turk, despite my cries of protest, Fritz seated the terrified monkey on the beast's back, securing it there with a cord and then putting a second string round the dog's neck that he might lead him. He put a loop of the knot into the little rider's hand, saying gravely, "Having slain the parent, Mr. Turk, you will please to carry the son."

This arrangement mightily displeased them both, but by and by they yielded to it quietly. Over time, the monkey became especially amused by it, riding along with the air of a person perfectly at his ease. Meanwhile, I could see in the eye of the dog that he was calculating how to flip the rider straight onto his tongue.

My son inquired as to what species of the monkey tribe I thought his protégé belonged, which, by taking my mind off the situation, eased some of my anxiety, and conversation ensued regarding whether or not monkeys had a soul. I spoke most of the walk with Fritz at intervals mumbling, "Seriously?" and "What did you smoke, again?" until we found ourselves on the rocky margin of the stream and close to the rest of our party.

CHAPTER 6

Back to the Tent We Call "Home," or Just "the Tent"

"If it be the will of Jah to leave us alone in this solitary place, let us be high as kites and rejoice with a toke of a marijuana cigarette."

Juno was the first to be aware of our approach and gave notice of it by barking loudly, to which Turk replied with such hearty goodwill that for a moment I forgot that he was the spawn of evil. His little rider, on the other hand, not fooled and terrified at the noise his steed was making, slipped from under the cord and fled to his refuge on Fritz's shoulder, where he regained his composure and settled himself comfortably.

Turk, who by this time knew where he was, and finding himself free, dashed forward to rejoin his friend and let her know the weaknesses he had spotted in us. One after another our dear ones came running to the opposite bank, testifying in various ways their delight at our return—my wife blew kisses and sent a telepathic message saying she couldn't wait to get some private time with me in the tent. Jack kept doing cowboy calls like, "Yippee kayay!" and "Yee haw!" whereas Ernest stood solemnly and sang in a Chet Baker tenor, "Fly Me to the Moon" for no other reason than that he was happy. We were quickly on the other side, and full of joy and affection, our happy party was once more united.

The boys, suddenly perceiving the little animal in alarm at the tumult of voices that was clinging close to their brother, shouted in ecstasy—but probably not *on* Ecstasy, "A monkey! A monkey! Awesome! Where did Fritz find him? What can we give him to eat?" Then, refocusing their limited attention, they chorused, "Look at those awesome branches of reefer Father has brought!"

We could neither comprehend this confused torrent of questions, nor get a word in edgewise to answer them.

At length when the excitement had subsided a little, I was able to say a few words. "I am truly thankful to see you all comfortably blotto and, thank Jah, our expedition has ensured we may remain so for as long as we'd like . . . not to mention, well fed." And I held up our bounty and handed a little of the reefer to my wife with which to load up a kick stick ASAP.

"If it be the will of Jah," said my wife, "to leave us alone in this solitary place, let us be high as kites and rejoice with a toke of a marijuana cigarette. I have been uneasy since you left even though you were only gone for the day, but now that I see you once more safe and well, I know how much of my anxiety was a side effect from the potlikker tea I've been drinking since I woke up this morning.

"Now we want to hear all your adventures, and let us relieve you of your burdens," she added, taking my cannabis stems.

Jack shouldered my gun, Franz took the coconuts, and Ernest took the monkey off his brother's shoulder. Fritz distributed the sugar cane among his brothers and handed Ernest his gun. Ernest, his eyes red as fire, found Fritz's "burden" too heavy to carry. His mother offered to relieve him of part of the load and took over the sugar cane, happily sucking the juice with vigor as soon as she could, her munchies getting the best of her. Franz gave up the coconuts to Jack but no sooner had he done so than his oldest brother exclaimed, "Hullo, Franz, you do not know what you are parting with. Are you really handing over those coconuts without so much as tasting them?"

"Are they really coconuts?" cried Franz, "I thought they were hairy baseballs!"

Everyone tried not to laugh, especially Fritz, who at one point, I pointed out, had thought them testicles.

"No, thank you," replied Jack with a smile when Franz tried to get them back. "I have no wish to see you overburdened again."

"Oh, but I have only to throw away these sticks, which are of no use, and then I can easily carry them," Franz assured him.

"Look again," I suggested. "I think you'd think those 'sticks' far less useless if you knew what Jah had sent you. Have you ever heard of rangoon?"

The words were scarcely out of my mouth when Ernest grabbed them and began to chew vigorously at the end of the branches like a pacifier.

"What is it?" asked Franz.

"Wild-grown marijuana," he explained between gnaws.

We went back to the camp and found preparations for a truly sumptuous meal. Several empty boxes of Ritz were strewn about, as were the discarded tins that had once contained lemon and olive oil soaked sardines. There were two forked sticks planted in the ground on either side of the fire, where on a rod hung several planks of Papa Dan's beef jerky crackling as it warmed in the flames. Franz gave the spit another turn, assuring me he had been helping out all day, but judging from his bloodshot eyes, I seriously doubted it. In the center sat the great pot from which issued the smell of a most delicious soup. To crown this sight stood a splendid array of Velveeta cheeses: a white one, a yellow one, and one with flecks of red stuff.

All this was very pleasant to two hungry travelers, but I was about to beg my wife to spare the jerky until we could make sure we had sufficient stock, when she, perceiving my telepathic thought, quickly relieved my anxiety. "This is not the beef jerky," she said, "but meat from a dead bird Ernest killed by accident when he was trying to fly off a tree branch and landed on it. We found the meat had dried out some in the sun after several hours and so we skinned it off and hung it over a fire."

"Yes," said Ernest, "it is a penguin, I think. Don't you think it must have been a penguin?"

"I have little doubt of the matter, my boy." I rolled my eyes off to the side so he wouldn't see and feel bad that this was as likely a penguin as I was Mary Poppins at the races. However, it was likely the boy had smoked away the vast majority of his brain matter, and we were frankly lucky he still spoke in English, unsure though we were of the dialect.

Looking again at the strange crackling meat, I found myself slightly concerned about allowing my family to actually ingest it. However, I was proud of my wife's creativity as we were going to have to make our snack foods last as long as possible, helpless as we were when it came to actually cooking.

And so we smoked the rangoon, to temper the wild and fishy flavor of the "penguin," as well as to improve the taste of the sardines. We did full justice to the meal prepared for us and no one became seriously ill. So I produced the coconuts for dessert.

"Here is better food for your little friend," I said to Fritz, who had failed at trying to persuade the monkey to taste morsels of the food we had been eating. "The poor animal has been accustomed to nothing but its mother's milk; fetch me a saw, one of you."

I then extracted the milk of the nuts from their natural holes. When I said, "I am now extracting the milk of the nuts from its natural holes," to my family, it made for a merry scene, which confused me tremendously. Enjoying the spirited laughter none-the-less, I carefully cut the shells in half. The monkey was perfectly satisfied with the milk and eagerly sucked the corner of a handkerchief dipped in it.

The sun was now rapidly sinking behind the horizon, and the poultry retiring for the night warned us that we must follow their example. Having offered up our prayers per the insistence of our eldest son, we lay down on our beds, with the monkey crouched down between Jack and Fritz, and we were all soon fast asleep.

We were not long asleep, however, when a loud barking from the dogs awakened us, and the fluttering and cackling of our poultry warned us that a foe was approaching. Fritz sprang up and, with the belligerence of a drunken bar bully, seized his gun and rushed out. Myself, the wife, and the other boys peeked our heads around the loose-hanging tent fabric. There we found a desperate battle going on; Fritz and the dogs, surrounded by a dozen or more large jackals, were fighting bravely, with four of their opponents dead, but the others remaining fearsome.

Fritz sent bullets through the heads of a couple more, a behavior I was beginning to doubt was solely about his withdrawal but might turn out to just be a thing with this kid. Meanwhile, the rest took the hint and galloped off. Turk and Juno did not intend that they should escape so cheaply, and pursuing them, they caught and likely turned the rest of the pack onto their case for island domination regardless of their near-fatal encounter. Fritz wanted to save one of the jackals to show his brothers in the morning. I told him that, if Turk and Juno were still hungry, we should give it to them as a peace offering. Fritz ignored me, which was fine because by then the dogs had curled up to sleep.

Soundly and peacefully we slept until the cock-crow, when my wife and I awoke. We shared a blunt followed by a quickie against some rocks down by the open ocean. Then we chilled for a while in the morning sun. Not wanting to do much more than that, I began to ruminate on all the remaining cool stuff still out on the shipwrecked boat.

"Return to the wreck by all means," agreed my wife, having heard my thoughts through my remarkable mental powers. "Patience, order, and perseverance will help us through all our hard work. A visit to the wreck is without a doubt our first duty. Come, let us wake the children, and set to work without delay."

They were soon roused, and Fritz having the smallest of the family's collective hangover, ran out for his jackal. It was cold and stiff from the night air (and rigor mortis), and he placed it on its legs before the tent, in a most life-like position, and stood by to watch the effect upon his brothers.

When the younger children emerged from the tent, many were the exclamations (to put it politely) they made at the sight of the strange dead animal.

"A yellow dog!" cried Franz.

"A wolf!" exclaimed Jack.

"It is a dancing girl," said Ernest—at which point everyone stopped to look at him in silence.

"Hullo," interrupted Fritz. "Who does not know a jackal when he sees one?"

"That 'hullo' thing you've started is annoying," said Jack, losing interest in the dead animal.

"But really," continued Ernest, examining the animal, "I think it is a lady in a golden tutu—she winked at me!" He giggled delightedly.

"Are you okay?" asked Fritz, examining his brother's eyes.

"Come on, boys," I interjected. "No more of this quarrelling. None of you are that far off (I couldn't bring myself to even glance at Ernest who was now making kissing sounds at the decomposing creature) for the jackal has similarities to all three—dog, wolf, and . . . er, well, dog and wolf."

Meanwhile, the monkey sat down on Jack's shoulder, but no sooner did it catch sight of Ernest trying to dance with the dead jackal, than it fled back into the tent, and hid itself in a heap of moss until nothing was visible but the tip of its little nose. Jack soothed and comforted the frightened little animal, and Fritz summoned us all to prayers, wondering if, seeing the state of his brother, we might not need them more than ever. Soon after, we began our breakfast.

So much had we eaten for our supper the previous night that we had little to eat but bags of corn nuts, which were so dry and hard, that, even hungry as we were, we could not swallow many. Fritz and I took some wine to help them down, while my wife and younger sons soaked theirs in brandy.

While we were thus employed, I noticed that the two dogs were lying unusually quietly by my side. I at first attributed this drowsiness to their having accepted us as their supreme rulers, but I soon discovered that it arose from a different cause; the animals had not escaped unhurt from their late-night combat but had received several deep and painful wounds, especially about the neck. The dogs began to lick each other on the places that they could not reach with their own tongues, and my wife carefully dressed the wounds with butter. I allowed her to do so even though I had no idea what kind of restorative properties were in butter—although I said, "Butter?"

And she said, "Yes."

And I said, "Do you mean snapdragon oil?"

And she answered, "No. I mean butter."

"One of the things we must not forget to look for on the boat," said Fritz, changing the ridiculous subject, "are spiked collars for each of the dogs, as protection for them should they again be called upon to defend themselves from wild beasts."

"Oh, yes," whispered Turk so that only I could hear, "you will make us armor so that when the battle begins, we will overtake you all easily."

I begged the party who were to remain onshore, to keep together as much as possible and to try to stay away from that mangy mutt. I reminded my younger sons to obey their mother in all things, and I arranged a set of telepathic signals with my wife that we might communicate at great distance. Fritz erected a signal-post by hoisting a strip of sailcloth as a flag. This flag was to remain hoisted so long as all was well on shore, but should our return be desired, three shots were to be fired, *away from all living things*, and the flag lowered. All the while Fritz could be heard mumbling about how telepathy was an enormous crock and it was important to have some real methods of communicating.

I allowed him to take whatever precautions he felt necessary, mostly because I didn't really care. I knew my way would have been just as effective, but, if he felt like hanging linen up on a pole, so be it.

Except for a substantial pot stash, and Fritz with his gun, we took little, so that we might leave as much space as possible to bring goods back with us. As a family, we lit up a see-ya-later doobie and agreed it best if no one expected us back for a few days, seeing as there was a lot of work to do out there and a lot of pot in the bag on my back.

CHAPTER 7

To the Shipwreck with a Monkey

*But by smoking enough reefer
to kill an eight-year-old child,
the night at length passed away.*

We had not gotten far from the shore, when I found that I was able to use telekinesis to establish a current from the river in direct line with the vessel, and though my nautical knowledge was not great, my powers were and I succeeded in steering the boat into the stream, which carried us nearly three-fourths of our passage with little or no effort. Then Fritz finished it off with a dint of hard pulling, (while I did my own pulling off a more refreshing "dint"), and we accomplished the whole distance.

First, we went to see to the animals who greeted us with joy—bellowing, bleating, and talking about their expectations for the upcoming Phish tour (which at first was funny because I thought they meant "fish").

The poor beasts were not hungry, for they were all still well supplied with food, but they were apparently pleased by the mere sight of human beings, which I felt would bode well for us when Turk's revolution began.

Fritz then placed his monkey by one of the goat's teats and the little animal immediately suckled the milk with evident relish, chattering and grinning all the while. The monkey provided for, we refreshed ourselves with a plentiful bowl—or at least I did, while Fritz took apart a coconut. "Now," said Fritz, "we have plenty to do. Where should we begin?"

"Let us build a mast and sail for our boat," I answered, then was speedily distracted by a box containing a shiny crystal chandelier that had been brought along for our journey as something at which we could stare. "I . . . the light, Fritz, it's a rainbow. . . ."

Quite startled by my lack of focus, Fritz demanded, "What makes you think about rainbows at so critical a time when we have so many necessities to attend to?"

"I must confess," I said, "that I find it very difficult to concentrate for so long a time on one thing when there are so many wonder . . . Fritz! Look! It's a Rubik's Cube!" and it is very likely my voice trailed off as I tried to make an all-red side.

Meanwhile Fritz was ruminating about the journey home and how we weren't going to have the same current we rode out on, but he lost me at the word *we*, which oddly enough had also been the first word of the statement.

"I noticed that the wind blew strong in my face, toward land," he was saying, "while the current continued to carry us out. Now, as the current will be of no use on our way back, you were right to think that we might take the wind supply in its place."

His suggestion roused me back to attention. I knew I would be able to command the wind to push us back home. I had all the right powers for that. "You have reasoned well, my boy," I replied. "Let us set to work at once."

Fritz chose a stout spar to serve as a mast and, having made a hole in a plank nailed across one of the tubs, secured it with stays.

He then discovered a lug-sail, which had belonged to one of the ship's lifeboats. This he hoisted, making our craft ready to sail. I begged Fritz to help me decorate the masthead with a red streamer and some sparkly sequins to give our vessel a more finished appearance. Smiling at this childish but natural vanity, he complied with my request. Then, while I packed another bowl, Fritz put together a rudder, so that he would be able to steer the boat. He did not seem to know that I had a remarkable propensity for mentally steering the boat.

While Fritz was thus employed, I began exploring the shore through the captain's telescope and announced that the flag was flying and all was well.

Fritz grabbed it out of my hand with no shortage of aggravation, perhaps because he was working on our boat and I was playing with a telescope. By then, so much time had slipped away, that we found we could not return that night, as I had wished. I signaled with ESP our intention to remain onboard, while Fritz did it with the signal he had set up. I then spent the rest of the time rolling and smoking an enormous panatella as big as my head, which was funny just to look at and made me laugh until tears were running in streams down my cheeks. Meanwhile, the kid had embarked on taking out the stones we had placed in the boat for ballast, and stowed in their place heavy articles that would be of value to us on the island. At this point, I am fairly certain I had started playing a tambourine to accompany my kazoo.

This ship had sailed for the purpose of supplying a young stoner colony. She therefore had onboard every conceivable article we could desire. Our only difficulty would be to make a wise selection. I felt pretty calm and sanguine that we would be able to return for more, but Fritz seemed less certain—another reason I was opposed to his newfound love of sobriety.

First, we gathered a large quantity of gunpowder and bullets, per Fritz and his newfound loathing of the peace and love with which his mother and I had raised him. I tried to get him to take the sparkly crystal chandelier, but he kept slapping it out of my hand and finally detached a single crystal for me to take in my pocket. He, meanwhile, added three guns, a set of nunchucks, and a whole armful of swords, daggers and knives. Appalled, I tried to bring a Gameboy and some soft velvet that we could rub on each other's cheeks for something fun to do. But Fritz was going on that we remember silverware and other necessary goods, along with kitchen utensils of all sorts.

Exploring the captain's cabin, I discovered a small wine cellar, which, if the captain had been present, I'd have certainly awarded him a high-five for forethought. Fritz, over at the stores, supplied us with beef jerky, a few cases of canned soups including an entire box of Cream of Mushroom and one of beans with bacon, a few boxes of macaroni and cheese, Jimmy Dean breakfast sandwiches, and a bag of Hershey's Miniatures. There was also wheat, along with a large quantity of seeds and vegetables with which we had no idea what to do. There was of course, an entire pantry of Hot Pockets and another of countless Hostess products. I also added to our loot a barrel of sulfur for matches, a few screens for our bowls, some string for creative pot growing (not to mention to dangle in front of Ernest, then pull away quickly), cordage, and as many water bongs as I could find.

Fritz reminded me that sleeping on the ground, even with all the leaves we were smoking, had been both cold and hard, and insisted we add to our cargo some hammocks, blankets, and animal-print Snuggies in zebra, cheetah, penguin, pig, frog, and rabbit.

All this—with nails, tools, and, of course, endless agricultural implements—completed our load and sank our boat so low that I would have probably refused to get in had Fritz not pointed out that the sea was totally calm and reminded me that with a life jacket, I was a pretty good swimmer.

Night drew on and a large fire, lighted onshore, showed us that all was well. I replied with ESP while Fritz replied superfluously by hoisting four ship's lanterns. The islanders responded with two shots we prayed had been directed skyward, even though I had heard telepathically that my original signal had already been perceived.

The ship was in so wretched a condition that even the teeniest tempest would definitely complete her destruction. Even though I thought it'd be fun to test it out, Fritz demanded that "for safety's sake" we sleep in our small boat, which he said appeared safer than the great vessel. So, with a repeat of my earlier panatella joint, we retired and Fritz finally shut up about safety and fell asleep.

For a while I could not sleep, the thought of my wife and children—alone and unprotected with those insane dogs—disturbed my rest. But by smoking enough reefer to kill an eight-year-old child, the night at length passed away. At daybreak Fritz arose and went back onto the ship. A little fuzzy, I joined him about an hour later and brought the telescope to stare at the shore, which was super fun. Fritz asked if I saw the flag. I had already done some telepathy and didn't need to see the flag so I just mumbled, "Mm-hmm." I kept watch on the land and saw the door of the tent open. My wife appeared and looked steadfastly toward us.

"Wife," I said, "you are smokin' hot and I can't wait to smoke up a fatty with you."

"Husband," she replied, "so are you and me, too."

Fritz, behind me, hoisted the redundant white flag, and in reply, the flag onshore was thrice dipped. I didn't let the boy see me roll my eyes.

"Father," Fritz said, "now that we have had a look at Mother, my next concern is for the animals on board. Let us try to save the lives of some of them, at least, and to take them with us."

"Would it be possible to make a raft," I suggested, "and get them all on it and in that way take them to shore?"

"But how can we get a cow and an ass," he said with a completely straight face, "not to mention a sow to get on a raft and once there to remain motionless and quiet? The sheep and goats might do it, since they are of a more docile temper. But for the larger animals, I am at a loss as to how to proceed."

"We could tie a long rope around the sow's neck," I now proposed, "and throw her into the sea. Her immense bulk will be sure to sustain her above water, and with the rope we can pull her behind us."

"An excellent idea," he replied, "but unfortunately I care the least about saving the pig." The boy, his mother and I had noticed, had always possessed Islamic-Judeo leanings in his spirituality.

I had an idea about how to proceed using my powers, but I let Fritz invent a solution since his sobriety would probably make his life otherwise pretty boring.

"Well," said Fritz, "I can think of nothing else, unless we make them swimming-belts."

"Really, my boy, that is a great idea. I am not even joking," I continued, as I saw him smile, "we may get every one of the animals ashore in that way!"

Fritz caught a sheep and proceeded to put our plan into execution. I got distracted by the yellow dancing bear who had offered me a bite of his caramel apple.

"Hurrah!" exclaimed Fritz, throwing the miserable animal bound by his half-baked contraption into the water. "We will treat them all like that."

I wasn't sure if he noticed that I didn't really do anything to help because I was trying to see if I could fit my index finger into a hole in one of the deck planks—but Fritz successfully caught up and bound each animal, and after tossing it into the water, he would commence cheering for himself, in which I sometimes thought to join.

This done, the whole herd was ready to go, and Fritz brought the donkey to one of the ports to be the first to be launched. After some maneuvering we got the ass into a "convenient position," and then, with a sudden heave . . . well, you get the idea.

Anyway, he floated away, followed by the cow, sheep, the blue and red bears, and the goats, followed by the yellow bear and a small tribe of table-fairies. The sow alone remained, seeming determined not to leave the ship—she kicked, struggled, and squealed so violently that I thought we should abandon her or at least try to mellow her out with a contact buzz. Indeed, Fritz had me try blowing smoke at her snout. Finally, after much trouble, we succeeded in sending her out of the port after the others, and once in the water, such was her energy that she quickly out distanced them, and was the first to reach the shore—I credit the Chronic.

We steered for shore, drawing our herd after us. I saw, now, how impossible it would have been for us to have succeeded in getting back to shore without the aid of my magical powers. The weight of the goods sank the boat so low in the water that we could never have rowed so great a distance. The sail, however, worked very well with the winds I was able to induce with my mind so that we could fully chow down on some buttermilk biscuits for a midday meal. Then, while Fritz amused himself with his "monkey," I took up my "pipe" and amused myself.

As I was thus engaged, a sudden shout from Fritz surprised me. But when I glanced up, there stood Fritz with his gun to his shoulder pointing it at a huge shark. The monster was making for one of the finest sheep. Just as he turned on his side to seize his prey and the white of his belly appeared, Fritz fired. As the shot took effect, our enemy disappeared, leaving a trace of blood on the calm water.

"Well done, my boy," I cried, "you will become a crack whore one of these days." What I had meant to say was "crack shot," which Fritz understood because of my telepathic clarification. His eyes sparkled at his success and my praise, and reloading his gun, carefully watched the water. But the shark did not appear again.

Steering the boat with my mind to a convenient landing place, I cast off the ropes that secured the animals and let them get ashore as best as they might.

There was no sign of my wife or other children when we stepped on land, but after a few moments they appeared and with a shout of joy ran toward us.

We were thankful to be reunited—and it felt so good. After asking and replying to a few preliminary questions, Fritz proceeded to release the herd from their swimming-belts. My wife astonished at our success, exclaimed, "How clever you are!"

"I am not the inventor," I replied. "The honor is due to Fritz. He not only thought of this plan for bringing off the animals, but saved at least one of them from a gnarly death." And I then told them how bravely he had encountered the shark, only losing my train of thought once when I recounted how the ribbon of blood the injured animal left in the water had actually looked like ribbon and how good a metaphor it was. My good wife, managing to follow my tangent quite well, was delighted with her son's success but declared that she would hate our trips to the vessel more than ever, knowing that such savage fish inhabited the waters.

Fritz, Jack, and I began the work of unloading our craft. Of course, this meant that Fritz pretty much single-handedly unloaded because Jack and I were having a hard time with knots. Franz, meanwhile, had climbed up on the ass and was riding it like crazy, which was hilarious on multiple levels.

"Come, my boy," I said between chortles, "no one must be idle here, even for a moment. You will have enough riding practice later. For now, you must dismount the ass immediately," which had all of us erupting into a new bout of hysterics.

Franz fell to the ground laughing. "But I have not been idle all day," he cried out. "Look here!" and he pointed to a belt around his waist. It was made of yellow skin in which he had stuck a couple of pistols and a knife. "And see," he added, "what I have made for the dogs. Here, Juno, Turk," the dogs came up at his call, but they were both giving me the hairy eyeball. Around their necks were collars of the same skin, in which were fastened nails that bristled around them in a most formidable manner.

"Uh-oh," I stammered. Turk raised his eyebrow as if challenging me to do anything about his new protective device. "Who helped you?" I asked, knowing full well that the dog had cajoled such fine weaponry from the child.

"Except in sewing," said my wife, "he had little assistance. As for the materials, Fritz's jackal supplied us with the skin, and the needles and thread came out of my wonderful Ron 'Pigpen' McKernan signed tie-dyed bag."

I cocked my head to see if she was lying. I mean, I knew that Pigpen was an original member of the Grateful Dead and that my wife had followed them from '78-'83 but the great organist was actually dead of cirrhosis by '73. But she seemed sincere so I agreed the signature looked authentic.

Fritz, meanwhile, reminded me that I was rather uneasy about outfitting the dogs in such dangerous contraptions. He clearly did not approve of the use of his jackal's hide and holding his nose, begged his little brother to keep at a distance. "Really, Franz," he said, "you should have cured the hide before you used it. The smell is disgusting. Don't come near me."

"It's not the hide that smells," Franz retorted. "It is the nasty jackal itself that you left in the sun."

"Now, boys," I said, taking a hit off the J Ernest had lit to calm my nerves, "no quarrelling here. Franz, help your brother drag the carcass into the sea, and if your belt smells, take it off and dry it better."

The jackal was dragged off, and we finished the work of unloading our boat—and by *we*, I mean Fritz.

When this was accomplished, we went to the tent, where finding no preparation for supper, I said, "Fritz, get us one of those Pepperidge Farm Chicken Pot Pies."

"Ernest," added my wife, smiling, "let's see if we can conjure up some eggs."

Fritz got out a pie and carried it to his mother triumphantly, while Ernest set before me a dozen white balls with parchment-like coverings.

"Bocce balls!" I said. "Well done, Ernest. This will be totally entertaining! Especially if we can play with the house rules where you get extra points for hitting your opponent."

My wife glanced from me to the boys, which, in retrospect, might have been out of anxiety or just outright confusion. "Turtle eggs, dear," she said patting my arm. "Later we will tell you about our adventures. For now let's see what these eggs will do toward making a good supper for us. With these and your pie, I do not think we shall starve."

Leaving my wife to prepare supper, we returned to the shore and brought up what of the cargo we had left there—and by *we*, I mean Fritz. After watching him collect the herd of animals (except for the sow who ran away—perhaps to join up with Turk and Juno—and the ducks and geese who deserted us for a nearby marshy swamp—or so they said), we returned to the tent.

The meal awaiting us was about as civilized a one as people on a desert island could get. My wife had improvised a table of a board laid across four barrels. On this was spread a white tablecloth, with knives, forks, spoons, and plates set for each person. A tureen of Cream of Mushroom appeared first, followed by an omelet, then slices of the pie, and finally a bottle of the captain's canary wine.

While we ate, I told my wife about our adventures and then begged she would be able to remember what she had done in my absence—"Because," I told her, "sometimes I think that when I'm not around, everything stops. This was particularly true when I was a child and I would stay home sick from school. I believed that while for me a day of cold packs and television had transpired, for all of those other children there had been nothing but a hole in time. But that's another story. Now what were we talking about again? Oh yeah. What did you do today . . . if anything at all . . . ?"

CHAPTER 8

The Big Bud Grove as Detailed by the Island's Resident Hottie

The boys and I enjoyed our midday bowl immensely in this glorious palace of grass.

"I will spare you a description," said my wife, "of the first day. Truth be told, I spent the time chowing down on a wig-out sandwich and obsessing about your progress and signals. I rose very early this morning, and after receiving your signal that you were all right, I replied to it, and then while the boys slumbered, I sat down and began to consider how our position could be improved with a few tokes off the one-hitter.

"'For it is perfectly impossible, Self,' I said to myself, 'to live much longer where we are now. The sun beats down burningly all the livelong day on this rocky spot. Our only shelter is this poor tent, beneath the canvas of which the heat is even more oppressive than on the open shore. Why shouldn't my boys and I exert ourselves as much as my husband and Fritz? Why shouldn't we also try to accomplish something useful?

"'If we could exchange this melancholy and unwholesome place for a pleasant shady dwelling, we would all be stoked. Among those delightful woods and marijuana groves where Fritz and his father saw so many charming things, I feel sure there must be some little retreat where we could establish ourselves comfortably. There must be, and I will find it.'

"By this time the boys were up, and I watched as Franz set to task on making his belt and dog collars with the 'help' of his brother Ernest. After they set the skins to dry, I proposed that a walk would do all of us some good.

"The boys went along with my scheme of a journey mostly because they were too afraid to stay by themselves because Ernest kept saying that he saw elves. Preparations were instantly made. We gathered weapons and provisions. The two boys carried guns—and Ernest carried a purse—while they gave me the water flask and a small hatchet to carry.

"Leaving everything in as good order as we could at the tent, and at the last minute remembering that we had almost forgotten Franz, we proceeded toward the stream, accompanied by the dogs. Turk, who had accompanied you on your first expedition, seemed immediately to understand that we wished to pursue the same route and led the way.

"As I looked at my two sons, each with his gun, and considered how much our safety depended on them, I felt grateful to Jah for understanding that while we truly believe in love and peace, sometimes it's good to have been acquainted with firearms.

"Filling our water-bong, we crossed the stream and climbed up to a higher point where, as you described, a lovely view can be obtained. The sight filled me with a pleasurable sensation of buoyant hope.

"A pretty little wood in the distance attracted my attention, and we went to check it out. But finding it impossible to force our way through the tall, strong, healthy grass crops that grew higher than the boys' heads, we turned toward the open beach to our left and followed it. Soon we reached a locale much nearer the little wood, at which point we turned inland and made our way toward it.

"We had not entirely escaped the tall grass, however, and with the utmost fatigue and difficulty from our respective buzzes, we were struggling through the fields, when suddenly a great rushing noise terrified us. A very large and powerful bird sprang upward. Both boys attempted to take aim, but the bird was far away before they were ready to fire.

"'That sucks!' exclaimed Jack. 'Now if I had had been carrying the light gun, and the bird hadn't flown so fast, I would have brought it down!'

"'Oh yes,' I agreed. 'No doubt you would be a great shot if your game gave you time to get ready.'

"'But I had no idea that anything was going to fly up at us like that,' he cried.

"'A good shot,' I replied, 'must be prepared for surprises. No wild birds or wild beasts will send you notice that they are about to fly or run your way.'

"'What sort of bird was it?' Franz asked.

"'Oh, it must have been an eagle,' answered Jack, 'it was enormous!'

"'So every big bird has to be an eagle?' replied Franz, in a tone of mockery.

"'Let's see where he was sitting, anyway,' I suggested.

"Jack sprang toward the place, and instantly a second bird, even larger than the first, rushed up into the air, with a most startling noise.

"The boys stood staring upward, perfectly stupefied, while I laughed uncontrollably and said, 'Well, you are most definitely first-rate hunters, my sons!'

"At this, Jack looked like he was going to cry, while Ernest bowed low and called after the bird, 'Adieu for the present, sir! I live in hopes of another meeting!' He had us all in stitches and even cheered up old Jack. Jack then noticed in the sky a large, but very dilapidated old tree house that soared high above the grove. 'What should we make of that?' he asked. As I was too foggy to trust that what he was seeing was actually there, I let his comment pass unattended and we kept giggling as we continued on our exploration.

"Finally, we approached the pretty overgrowth. Birds fluttered and sang among the high stems, and I asked the boys not to try to shoot any of the happy little creatures. We nearly broke into chorus in our admiration of this beautiful marijuana grove. I cannot describe to you how wonderful it is, nor can you form the least idea of its enormous size without seeing it for yourself—unlike that rundown old tree house, this was no hallucination. What we had been calling 'a wood' proved to be an inexhaustible supply of healthy, flowering marijuana plants, and, what was strange, the roots sustained the massive leaves high in the air, forming strong arches all around each individual stem.

"I gave Jack some twine, and scrambling up one of the heartier stalks, he succeeded in measuring the largest leaf we could find, and figured it as wide around as an elephant ear. The flowers were large and abundant, throwing delicious smells all around us. The ground too was carpeted with soft green herbage. It is the most charming resting-place there ever was, and the boys and I enjoyed our midday bowl immensely in this glorious palace of grass.

"The dogs joined us after a while. They had stayed behind at the seashore. I was surprised to see them lie down and go immediately to sleep without even begging for food.

"The longer we remained in this enchanting place, the more I loved it. If we could live in some sort of dwelling among these grand, noble specimens, I should feel perfectly safe and happy. It seemed to me absurd to think we could ever find another place half so lovely, so I decided to search no farther and return to the beach to see if anything from the wreck had been brought up by the waves, to carry away with us.

"On reaching the shore, we found many articles strewn about of little value but all too heavy for us to lift, regardless. So instead we rolled some doobies and watched the dogs play among the rocks. Soon our munchies got the best of us as we saw that the dogs were carefully watching the crevices and pools, and every now and then they would pounce downward and seize something that they swallowed with relish.

"'They are eating crabs,' Jack pointed out. 'No wonder they have not seemed hungry lately.'

"And, sure enough, they were catching the little green crabs, plentiful in the water.

"Some time afterward, just as we were about to turn inland, we noticed that Juno was scraping in the sand and turning up something round, which she hastily devoured.

"Jack went to see what they were, and reported calmly that the dog had found turtle eggs.

"'Oh,' I cried, 'then let us share in the booty! I know how to make scrambled eggs!'

"Juno, however, did not at all approve of this, and with some difficulty, we finally drove her aside while we gathered a few dozen eggs, stowing them in our provision bags. Just then, we caught sight of a sail that appeared to be merrily approaching the shore beyond the cliffs. Franz knew it was you. But Ernest, always having the fear of savages, looked frightened, and for a moment I, too, was met with the beginnings of a full-on wig-out.

"We went to the stream and stepped on stones to cross it. It was then that we came in sight of the landing-place, where we joyfully met you and not, like, *Deliverance*.

"Now I hope you approve of our exploration and that tomorrow you will do me a favor and pack up everything, and take us away to live among my splendid weeds."

CHAPTER 9

Building a Bridge Is Less Fun than Getting High and Watching *Sanford and Son*

"I do not know what kind of plan it is to live in a smokable house."

B y the time my gorgeous wife had finished her speech,
she was flushed and wide-eyed.

"My little wife," I said. "Is that your idea of comfort and
security? Some weeds? I do not know what kind of plan it is
to live in a smokable house. If we were a family of Rizlas, we
could roll it all up and it would be an excellent plan."

"Laugh as much as you like," returned my wife, "my idea
is not as absurd as you make it sound. We should be safe in
there, camouflaged and comforted. I know on vacation in
Jamaica, I have seen pretty homes with strong floors, made
of bamboo rods and palm, and they seemed a fine place to
spend time. Why can't we build a natural place like that
where we could sleep happily at night?"

"I will consider the idea seriously, my wife," I said.
"Maybe something will come of it after all! Meanwhile,
since we have finished our supper and night is coming on,
let us toke in honor of the great Jah's protection and then
pass out."

Beneath the shelter of our tent, we slept soundly until
dawn when my wife and I woke up and snuck away to our
lovemaking rock down on the beach.

Afterward, when she thought I was nicely buttered up,
she referred me back to the task she had proposed the previous evening. I told her that to undertake it would involve so
much work that we would probably have to smoke a bowl
on the matter and weigh the probability that we wouldn't
even get around to it.

"First of all," I began, "I am not so quick to leave a
place to which I am pretty sure we were led by Jah and my

telepathic powers as a landing-place. See how secure it is guarded on all sides by these high cliffs and accessible only by the narrow passage to the fjord? And from this point, it is so easy to reach the ship that all of its valuable cargo is at our disposal. If we decide to stay here patiently, we can at least make sure we have brought everything onshore that we possibly can."

"I agree with you to a certain extent, dear husband," she replied with a gentle hand on my arm, "but you have no idea how dreadfully the heat off the rocks gets to me. It is almost intolerable while you and Fritz are away out at sea or wandering among the shady woods where it is cool and refreshing.

"As for the contents of the ship, a lot of it has already come ashore, and I would rather give up the rest to be spared the painful anxiety of your . . . er . . . *powers* . . . at some point failing to get you either to or from—not to mention the unbearable heat with which I must myself contend."

"Well, I admit, you have a point." I offered, "Suppose we went to your chosen living quarters, and left this rocky location as our place of retreat in case of danger. I could easily render it even more secure, by blasting portions of the rock with gunpowder." I shuddered with excitement at the prospect of blowing things up and then continued, "But a bridge must be built to enable us to cross back and forth with ease."

"Oh, I don't know if I won't drop dead of heatstroke before we can leave this place if I must wait for you to build a bridge!" cried my wife impatiently. "Let's just take our things on our backs and wade across the water as we have done a thousand times already! The cow and donkey can carry a great deal."

"They'll have to do that no matter how we make the move," I said, "but we still need bags and baskets to put things in. If you will focus on figuring out how to manufacture those, I will get going on the bridge. We need one anyway since the stream will probably swell and become impassable at times."

"Well, well!" cried my wife, clearly distraught at the idea that her grove would have to wait a while longer. "I submit to your argument, but please start building and don't make this another 'Dude, if I just dig this hole a little deeper and throw down a layer of cement we'll have a swimming pool!' as you did when I was pregnant with Fritz. You left me with a giant hole in my backyard for twenty-three years!"

With that, my precious wife stormed away and left me deep in thought about the nature of bridge construction as I puffed on my pipe and watched the water lap the shore. Of course, in no time, my thoughts were back to blowing shit up. "Gunpowder is indeed the most dangerous and, at the same time, the most entertaining thing we have," I mumbled to myself. "I will start by blowing up part of the cliff. . . ."

By the time the children were awake and hearing about the proposed move, my wife had woven several baskets and Fritz had started making harnesses for the animals to carry goods across the island. Meanwhile, I had done some really cool shit with gasoline and coconut rinds.

After eating a filling breakfast of cold Hot Pockets and a Twinkie, I noticed that everyone was engaged in some useful activity. So I proposed a boat ride. Instead, Fritz thought it would be more productive to make our way back to the wreck in order to obtain planks for the proposed bridge I forgot I had proposed. Now it just seemed silly.

Both Ernest and Fritz accompanied me on my boat ride. Soon I had managed to use my powers to guide us into a happy current and we were carried swiftly out to sea. Fritz thought he was steering with the rudder he'd built, so I let him think it. We had no sooner passed beyond the entrance of the bay when we were amazed to see countless multitudes of seabirds, gulls and others, that rose like a cloud into the air as we approached. Their wild and screaming cries nearly deafened us. At first I thought they were congregating there by order of Turk in order to organize a plan to overtake my family, but then I saw that they were just birds—the normal kind.

Fritz would have started shooting at them if I had permitted it. I was curious to see what the great attraction might be for this swarm of feathered fowl, so using my powers to induce a fresh breeze from the sea, I directed our course toward the island.

"Aha, now I see what they are after!" said Ernest. "They have a huge monster-fish there! We must run for our lives! Run, I say!"

With that the boy began to paddle back and forth wildly as though being chased by an invisible demon. Fritz tried to subdue him with force, whereas I successfully subdued him with a giant spliff of peaceful, albeit paradoxically named, AK-47.

When we got Ernest singing show tunes quietly to himself underneath a towel, Fritz said, "There was nothing on this sandy beach when we passed yesterday, I am certain, Father."

"Why, Fritz!" cried Ernest, popping out from his hiding place and nearly giving me a heart attack, "it must be the shark! Your shark, you know! From yesterday."

"You are right, Ernest," I agreed, "although I think your imagination will run away with you if you don't lie back down. You'll look over and only see the pecking and tearing of the voracious birds. You'll just look at those terrific jaws, beneath the strange projecting snouts. You'll see the rows upon rows of murderous teeth!" Over time I became so lost in my speech that Fritz had to impart my remedy for Ernest to me.

So subdued was I that soon Ernest and I sat together on the floor of our respective tubs clapping our hands in a cheerful rendition of Miss Mary Mack: "Miss Mary Mack, Mack, Mack, lives in a sack, sack, sack . . ." we sang, while Fritz guided the boats safely to the ship where he detached some broad planks with his knife and returned us toward home.

As we sailed along, I sat well pleased with our lovely boat ride, while Fritz cast dirty looks in the direction of his wasted brother and me.

In order to show the young sober chap that I was still in my right mind, I began a discussion about how we might use the hide of the shark as sandpaper.

"The best leather sandpaper," I continued, "is prepared in Turkey, Persia, and Tartary, from the skins of horses and asses." Both boys laughed appreciatively. "It is useful in polishing wood joints. In France it is made from the rough skin of a hideous creature called the angel-fish."

"Angel-fish!" exclaimed Ernest, whooping up a wild laugh. "What a name to give to anything 'hideous,' Father!"

"There are bad angels as well as good ones," observed Fritz, in his dry, sober way.

I tried not to let him see Ernest and me roll our eyes at each other.

Meanwhile Fritz stopped at the carcass to fillet off several long pieces of the animal's hide. He hung it with nails from the mast to dry in the wind.

When we made it close to the shore, we lowered the sail and soon had our craft safely moored to the bank.

No one was in sight, not a sound to be heard, so all together we gave a loud cheery "Hallooooo," which after a while was answered in shrill tones, and my wife with the two boys came running from behind the high rocks between us and the stream, carrying small bundles in handkerchiefs.

When the mysterious bundles were opened, a great number of fine crawfish were displayed, making great efforts to escape by scuttling away in every direction. They were placed in a heap on the ground, which brought immeasurable fun and laughter for a really long time as we all chased them and had races. Franz named one "Gaylord," which made us all laugh and laugh.

"Now, Father, did we not do well, today?" cried Franz. "Have you ever seen such splendid crawfish? Oh, there were thousands of them! And I think we have two hundred here at least. Just look at their claws!"

"And who was the discoverer of these fine crabs, Franz?" I asked.

"Fancy Jack was the lucky man!" he answered. "We went for a walk toward the stream to look for a good place for the bridge. Jack got distracted by shiny pebbles and alabaster because he'd smoked so much rangoon, and you could strike sparks with them in the dark, which he did for more than an hour."

"'Franz! Franz!' Jack cried out, 'Come and see the crabs on Fritz's jackal!' That's where we threw it, and it was swarming with these creatures. Are you glad we found them, Father? Will they be good to eat?"

"Very excellent, my boy, if only we knew how to cook them. But they will make fine amusement."

We all sat down for an afternoon toke. Each party relayed his day's adventures while the wife passed out Cracker Jacks and peanut-butter crackers. We then went to bring our planks to land—and by *we*, I mean Fritz.

Jack showed me where he thought the bridge should go, and I certainly saw no better place, as the banks were close to each other at that point, steep, and of about equal height.

"How do we find out if our planks are long enough to reach across?" I wondered out loud.

"We should use a ball of string, Father!" said Ernest, already tangled up in one of his mother's colorful balls of yarn from her knitting kit.

"Tie one end to a stone," suggested Fritz, "and throw it across; then draw it back, and measure the line!"

"Or play Chinese jump rope!" offered Ernest.

Adopting my older son's idea, we figured the distance across to be eighteen feet. Then allowing three feet more at each side, we calculated twenty-four feet as the necessary length of the boards—or again, that would be Fritz's handiwork as the rest of us became fixated on a zany group of ants battling a mountainous crumb of Combos cheddar cheese stuffed pretzel.

The question of how to lay the planks across was a difficult one. So we decided to go get some snacks. As we sat resting afterward, my wife showed me her needlework. With hard labor and a little bit of Afghani Goo (for focus), she had made two large canvas bags for the ass to carry, which she said out loud so everyone had a good chuckle. Having no suitable needle, she had to bore out the hole for each stitch with a nail. We were all impressed by her ingenuity. Sometimes I forgot that my wife was as intelligent as she was the pinnacle of sexification.

We took our time with dinner since no one was particularly eager to continue the engineering work. We smoked a bunch of bowls while Fritz, and his newly adopted sour countenance, went for a walk to stare at the bridge some more.

He discovered, while there, that there were trees close to the stream on either side. While we were blotto on the other side of camp, my boy attached a rope near one end of a beam and slung it loosely over a tree. Then, fastening a long rope to the other end, he crossed with it over rocks and stones. By using this pulley system, we later learned he was able to arrange the rope on a strong limb of the opposite tree.

With one plank set across the stream, Jack and Ernest, having wandered off after what they called "invisible spectra," ran back to inform us all that the bridge was made!

When I arrived at the river, that industrious boy of mine had laid a second and third plank beside the first; and then he carefully secured these at each end to the ground and to the trees. He quickly sawed short boards and laid them side by side across the beams, with the other boys nailing them down lightly (with only one injury quickly fixed by the skinned-up J their mother had prepared for just such a happenstance)—and when this was done, our bridge was pronounced complete.

Nothing could exceed the excitement of the children. They danced around singing "All That She Wants," by Ace of Base, shouting and making a general ruckus. I must confess I hummed along and cut a little rug myself.

Now that the work (and celebratory dance party) was done, everyone was overcome with fatigue, and gladly returned to the tent for herbal refreshment and sleep.

CHAPTER 10

To the Weeds

I decided then that my family and I would try each strain alone and in varying combinations over time in order to find the World's Greatest High.

The next morning, while we breakfasted, I was making a little speech to my sons on the subject of baseball as a better overall pastime since it was both fun to watch and play, while one can really only enjoy *watching* football due to its inherent danger—when my wife and Fritz interrupted me to go over the important move we were about to make and pointed out that it would require caution and focus from us all.

"Remember," Fritz said, "that, even though you have all begun to feel at ease here, we are still complete strangers to a variety of threats that may surprise us out of nowhere."

"I ask you, therefore," my wife put in, oddly staring directly at me, "to maintain good order and keep together on the march. No darting off. No lingering behind to philosophize. And now all hands to work."

Activity, though sluggish, began. Some collected provisions; others packed kitchen utensils, tools, ropes, and hammocks and arranged them as burdens for the cow and donkey.

My wife asked for a seat on the ass for her little Franz, which made everyone laugh. Then she assured me that she couldn't leave behind the poultry, even for a night, nor exist without her magic tie-dye bag. I agreed to do my best to please her, without provoking downright cruelty to the animals.

The children ran off to catch the cocks—and hens. Great chasing, fluttering, and cackling ensued but with no success, until my wise wife scattered some grain within the open tent. Soon the decoyed fowls and pigeons made their way into the enclosure, where, when the curtain was dropped, they were easily caught, tied together, and placed on the cow.

Franz was firmly seated on the donkey, while all sorts of bags and bundles rose about him like cushions and pillows, and his curly head rested on the wife's magic bag. Having filled the tent with the things we left behind, and closing it carefully, we were finally ready to go, each well equipped and in the highest spirits from the sweet smoky high on which we were all, but one, afloat.

Fritz and his mother led the way. Franz on his ass followed them closely.

Jack conducted the goats. On the back of one of them rode Nips the monkey, named of course for the other kind of nips—Cheese Nips—a favorite family snack we had all been sorely missing.

The sheep were under Ernest's care, and by the halfway point, they had all gone missing as had Ernest. I brought up the rear carefully watching the two dogs who kept constantly running backward and forward among us to keep a steady, if suspicious, eye on our party.

"We seem like one of those delightful tribes," said Ernest, reappearing sheepless but oddly holding onto a bouquet of peacock feathers, "shifting from place to place, without any wish to settle. . . ."

"Yes," I agreed, happy to take my mind off the evil thoughts of our big, cruel dog. "Among the Arabs, Tartars, and some other Eastern nations, this mode of life is natural. They, for that reason, are called nomads. They use camels and horses and a wonderful little refreshment known as hashish to move steadily from place to place. But I suspect your mother and I will be satisfied with only one such undertaking, especially since we lack the mythical black tar of Arabia to help relieve our burden."

It's true, our pace was slow and stoned, and so we had only come upon Fritz's bridge. His mother offered him well-merited praise for his skill in its construction, and we passed over it in grand procession. On the opposite side we discovered our batty old sow. The creature had resisted our attempts to bring her with us but, finding herself deserted, had followed of her own accord, testifying in the most unmistakable manner her entire disapproval of our proceedings. Meanwhile, I was impressed that Turk had taught her to speak, although no one else seemed interested by it in the least.

Fritz soon found we had to, as before, turn down to the beach, for the rank grass impeded our progress and also tempted the rest of us from the task at hand. He didn't want to lose any more of us or our livestock as we had already managed to lose.

We were making good time, when both the dogs suddenly left to plot against us, and a furious barking, followed by howling, erupted from the direction they had gone.

"It's the fish-monster," Ernest exclaimed, looking ashen and weak.

However, Fritz cocked his gun and advanced boldly. Ernest, meanwhile, passed out cold. So Jack hurried after Fritz without so much as unslinging his gun from his shoulders.

I thought it best if I stayed back with my wife who was tending to Ernest when I heard Jack shouting excitedly:

"Father! Father! Come quickly! A huge porcupine! A most enormous porcupine!"

Sure enough, the dogs were rushing around and around a porcupine, calling to it to join them when the revolution came.

I was therefore amused, when, while we were looking at the curious creature, little Jack stepped close to it, and with a pocket pistol in his hand, shot it dead, making sure of it by issuing a few hearty raps on the head. Sundry attempts to move it resulted in bloody fingers, till Jack, taking the handkerchief from his head and fastening one corner round the thing's neck, ran off, dragging it after him to where his mother awaited us.

"Hey, Mother! Look at this beast! I shot it, and it's good to eat! I only wish you had seen how it terrified the dogs." This remark caused a momentary growl from Turk and a haughty "Ha!" from his mate.

Ernest, awakening to the creature, pronounced its incisor teeth, its ears, and its feet to resemble those of his aunt Marjorie, pointing out the curious crest of stiff hairs on its head and neck.

"Oh, please, can we take it? Maybe it's good to eat!" said Jack, although Ernest turned pale and gagged momentarily upon gasping, "But it's Aunt Marjorie!"

However, given the younger child's eagerness, and wanting to please him even though I knew we'd never figure out how to prepare the thing safely for eating, I bundled it awkwardly, wrapping it in several folds of cloth, and added it to the donkey's load.

Our party then decided it was seriously time to smoke up. After resting, and comparing early Michael Jackson to contemporary British rock, we were encouraged by a frustrated Fritz to resume our march, which continued steadily, until we came in sight of our future place of residence.

What made this place different than the other abundant groves of marijuana we had come across on the island was the sheer size of these plants. Hearty and strong, their leaves were almost rubbery in their density. The colors of the crystals on every stem gleamed with all the colors of the rainbow. Their wonderful appearance filled each of us with a calm beauty and was fully deserving of the enthusiastic description it had been given. My wife gladly heard me say that if a dwelling could be contrived from the branches, it would be the happiest, highest, and most chillin' home in the world.

Fritz hastily unloaded, while the rest of us wandered in and out of the glorious plants.

The doves and poultry were set at liberty, and we all sat down to rest among the soft herbage while we laid our plans for the night.

Fritz saw little reason to stay and relax and presently left us, but soon two shots were fired and he appeared again holding a fine tiger over his shoulder, which, all of us thought incredibly cruel.

"Dude, what is up with that?" moaned Jack.

"I do believe those lovely animals are on an endangered species list," I added.

"I figured we wouldn't want our cocks on an endangered species list—not to mention hens and goats," he answered testily. "I just hope he doesn't have any companion near at hand."

We all shuddered at the thought.

"It's weird," remarked Ernest, "that Jah has created scary animals like this."

"Circle of life," Fritz mumbled under his breath as he went off to skin his kill.

"Animals prey upon one another as a means of preserving a due balance in the world of nature," agreed my awesome and beautiful hippie wife.

"Well, this one most certainly belongs to a fierce and bloodthirsty race," I sagely imparted. "Tigers are native to India, but I guess a few somehow made their way to this island that also seems to host penguins, flamingos, monkeys, and porcupines, but that's something to discuss another day. Regardless this would have proven a cruel foe, not only of our poultry, but also of our sheep and goats. I am well pleased that Fritz has rid us of it."

After the excitement, everyone scattered to do his or her own thing. Ernest was skipping from large flat stone to large flat stone, shrieking that he didn't want to fall in. No one knew what he meant, but Franz and Jack began gathering up Ernest's stones to form a fireplace, while I gathered sticks as their mother began to prepare some snacks.

"What kind of bambalacha do you think this is, Father?" asked Jack, seeing me examining the plant under which we were sitting. "Doesn't it smell like roasted walnuts?"

"There is a resemblance, but in my opinion these gigantic plants must be Big Bud or a relative of the Northern Lights strain. I have heard their enormous leaves described, and also the peculiarity of the sticky buds that allow support to the unusually large stems, not to mention the earthy smell you have here likened to walnut."

Just then little Franz came up with a large bundle of leaves, and his mouth full of something that he was eating with evident satisfaction.

"Oh, Mother!" he cried. "This is so good! So delicious!"

"Greedy little boy!" she exclaimed in fright. "What have you got there? Don't swallow it, whatever you do. It will make you lose your mind! Did you see all those crystals? Spit it all out this minute!" And the anxious mother quickly extracted from the boy's mouth the remains of a small fig.

"Where did you find that?" I asked.

"There are thousands lying among the grass over there," he replied. "They taste very nice. Do you think these will hurt me? The pigeons and the hens are gobbling them up with all their might!"

"I think you have no cause for alarm, dear wife," I said. "There must be some giant fig trees nearby that would make for an excellent base for a tree house. But look around. These plants, already in bricklike clumps, would make far better digs, if I had to choose."

My wife now continued her preparations for dinner. The porcupine was put on the fire to boil, but wasn't smelling too good. Luckily my wife had mastered a cooking technique whereby she crushed up a box of Ritz and then added water and a chicken egg to make dough. By squeezing string cheese over the top and adding pieces of salami, she had managed to invent a fairly delicious pizza, which was heating on a plank over the fire.

I took the boiling porcupine from its bath in order to harvest its quills as cleaning devices for our pipes and bowls as the sticky resin was quickly building up. The red-hot nail I had employed to pry them free, however, led to a rash of blisters in various sizes that reminded me of an incident with a co-ed from before I was married. So I moved on to smoking more of our plentiful and ever-growing stash of nearly every strain of marijuana known to man.

That's when it hit me: I decided then that my family and I would try each strain alone and in varying combinations over time in order to find the World's Greatest High.

We would start immediately. We examined the different species and chose one that seemed like the best with which to begin our experiments. A purple bud of Ice met each of our needs nicely—when who else but my sober child piped up with, "You won't be able to measure that way."

"What? Who asked you? Is that Mickey Mouse?" we asked in no particular order.

"I'm just saying that you should start in the morning when you are all *basically* sober and then each of you should smoke the very same amount such that you are in essence sharing the same experience. Then you need to keep records, so that you don't forget your experiences as they happen— the type of ganja in which you have partaken, how much, and when—I mean, if you want to be scientific about it."

We all sat looking upon my firstborn with minds full-blown. He was right! That was the only way to conduct our study! Everyone agreed and told me so telepathically as the smart child continued. "For now we should really figure out how we're going to build a house out of this mess."

The leaves spread a fair height above us, and I made the boys try to throw string or ropes around them, my intention being to get them all stuck together so that we might carve out walls.

Finding we did not succeed in this way, I kicked about other schemes in my mind, while I went with Jack and Franz to gather a pot of water from the small brook close by. I showed them how to place the leaves to steep and soften in the water, with stones placed on them to keep them beneath the surface. This would make a lovely refreshment once we allowed it to cool and added honey.

Then, of course, exhausted from this exercise, we ate dinner and prepared our night quarters. I slung our hammocks from the roots of a nearby tree, which formed an arched roof, and covered it all with cloth from the ship's sail, thus making a temporary tent, which would at least keep out the night dampness and noxious insects that had me beyond terrified. . . .

CHAPTER 11

To the Weeds, Continued . . . or, Just, IN the Weeds

As Fritz set about manufacturing his magic ladder, the boys and I decided to pack up a bowl and sing a few easy-listening hits . . .

Excited by the prospect of the next day's experiment, and completely out of character, sleep wouldn't come easily, so I roused my groggy family before sunrise—with caffeinated and spiked liquid encouragement, of course—to get started building our new home. After some Lucky Charms in coconut milk, I walked down with Fritz and Ernest to the beach to look for wood suitable for erecting our new abode but was quickly separated from them by a beam of light I was certain had begun chasing me.

Ernest, on the other hand, collected some lovely decorative driftwood we decided to use in the atrium of our future residence. We then took to choosing the bud we planned to smoke from our ever-increasing stash for our science experiment. The red crystals of the Hydroponic we had found in a nearby Hydrofarm, Ernest declared, had once made him see the world as if it were entirely made of gold.

While a group of pink and snow-colored flamingos rushed the sky and Fritz shot one for sport, Ernest and I prepared five equal joints of Hydroponic in preparation for our experiment to begin.

My wife tried for a while to prepare the bird's carcass for supper later, then gave up and buried it when she thought no one was looking. The other children began cutting down stalks of the Big Bud species in which we deigned to live. Harvesting giant bundles at a time, they packed it together, binding it tightly with the twine we had brought off the ship.

"What are you doing?" I exclaimed. "Have you done much damage? Can it still be smoked if dried?"

"These crystals are so sticky, nearly as good as any concrete," remarked Fritz. "They will make fine solid bricks if well packed."

"Yes," agreed Ernest, "and that stalk over there is named Timmy and loves dancing and Connect Four by candle light." With that, we lost Ernest to a far corner of the grove.

"Well," said Fritz, clearing his voice and casting his eyes to the ground, "we have our work cut out for us if we want to make enough bricks to construct a dwelling suitable for life on this island."

Fritz and the other boys then began to carry piles of the harvested stems back to our temporary quarters, while I, having been brought around to my good son's way of thinking, proceeded to cut more. I chose those that had flowered, knowing that they were more durable, and having cut a sufficient quantity of these, I selected one or two of the tallest plants I could find as central support beams. I then bound them all together and returned to my family.

When I arrived, my stoner sons were endeavoring to figure out the height of the lowest branch of the tree under which we were encamped. They had fastened together two long reeds and were trying to measure the distance, but in vain—they soon found that they were ten times more blitzed than anyone attempting the use of their right brain can technically get away with being.

"Hello, my boys," I said, when I discovered what they were doing, "is this some kind of a game? Why are you playing with numbers when you could be breaking out the bongo drums and singing 'Ewok Celebration'!"

"It was Fritz's idea," explained my youngest. "He thinks our house will be better if it has levers … multigrain … multigrain levers? No … what does it need to have again, Fritz?"

"Multi-levels," Fritz called from the other side of the tree with no secret to his exasperation. "Geometry will simplify the operation considerably," he went on, showing off as he met us on our side of the tree. "With its help, the altitude of the highest mountains can be ascertained—we may, therefore, easily find the height of this one branch."

With that, Fritz measured out a certain distance from the base of the tree and marked the spot, and then by means of a rod, whose length he knew, and imaginary lines, he calculated the angle of the trunk of the tree from the ground to the root of the branch. In this way, he was able to discover magically the height of the branch and, to the astonishment of the rest of us, announced that we would in part live thirty feet above the ground. This he told us he wanted to know so that he could construct a ladder of the necessary height.

As Fritz set about manufacturing his magic ladder, the boys and I decided to pack up a bowl and sing a few easy-listening hits like "Baby I'm-a Want You" and "Woman in Love." However, after the move and so many dazzling experiences, no one could find a bowl anywhere. So, to showcase my ingenuity, I took a strong piece of bamboo and bent it until it split into a single small piece. Then, using a knife, I carved a hole out of a leftover coconut rind. Fitting the bamboo rod into the hole, I sealed it with the sap oozing from Fritz's tree. It was messy, however, so I then wrapped the entire pipe with a large mangrove leaf. The boys saw what I had done and were delighted, and begged to have the pleasure of taking the first hit.

"No, no!" I said, "I did not make this for mere pleasure, nor is it even intended as a true pipe. Elizabeth," I said to my wife, using her first name for the first time in eleven chapters, "can you supply me with one of those wonderful screens you remembered in your magical bag?"

"Certainly," she replied, "I think that I have one right here," and diving her hand deep in, she drew out the very thing I wanted.

"Now, boys," I said, "I am going to show you how this contraption works," and first I poured water from a nearby jug into the empty coconut rind. Thus was the first step in my undertaking accomplished. Then I laid my dear Elizabeth's screen over top, needing only to trim it slightly since it had come out of one of the higher portholes of the ship, thanks to my wife's foresight.

The contraption worked quite well—but for the fact that being somewhat large and cumbersome, required that each person hold his own bowl while another lit it. After each of us had enjoyed his or her fill of a large and satisfying evening toke, we forgot the songs we had intended to sing and instead watched Jack and Franz wrestle while Ernest played bongos and told a story about a man who fell in love with a life jacket.

In all this time, Fritz had obtained two coils of cord each about forty feet in length and had stretched them out on the ground side by side. Then he cut bamboo into pieces of two feet for the steps of the ladder, and as he handed them to me, I passed them to his mother who passed them to Franz who passed them to Jack who passed them to Ernest who started to suck on them. Giving up this method, Fritz went back to work on his own. When the ladder was finished, he managed to find a rope by which it might be hauled up. Using a bow he had made from solid bamboo, he shot a rock tied with one end of the rope attached to a bamboo arrow over a branch. This done, he then fixed the lower end of the ladder firmly to the ground by means of stakes, and so it was ready for an ascent. The other boys and I who had been watching him with intense interest were each eager to be the first to climb the tree.

"Jack shall have the honor," Fritz said, "since he is not as fat as the rest of you. Just please do not break your neck."

Jack, who was as active as a monkey and resembled one given his ears and the shape of his head, sprang up the ladder and quickly gained the top.

"Three cheers for our new home!" he exclaimed, waving his cap.

"Hurrah, hurrah, hurrah for our jolly nest!!" we all exclaimed laughing at the fact that we were going to build a house out of marijuana, which was just too awesome for words and had likely directly led to our collective use of the word *jolly*.

Fritz, deciding to exploit our limited and tenuous enthusiasm, now called for a pulley, which my wife fastened to a cord hanging beside the ladder. I hauled it up, and finding the boys—who were now hanging from the branches—in my way, I told them to get down while I fastened the pulley to a stout branch above me, that we might be able to haul up the bricks we would require the next day. This reminded me that we would have to make a lot of bricks—and since a bright moon had recently arisen, by its light we began working on harvesting and bundling the pot into the hard bricks we would need until we were each quite worn out.

I looked around and to my surprise found that none of my boys were anywhere to be found. A moment afterward, however, all my anxiety was dispelled, for among the topmost boughs I heard their young voices raised in the evening hymn, "In da Church" by Diamond D.O.G, the spiritual knock off of 50 Cent's hip-hop classic "In da Club."

While I was busy, they had climbed upward, and had been sitting in silent admiration of the moonlight scene high above me. They soon came down and my wife showed us all the results of her labor and the two Adderall she had taken from the captain's medicine chest. She had created sixteen substantial piles of tightly woven bricks of marijuana. I congratulated her upon her success, and we then sat down to supper. On a cloth spread out upon the grass were arranged six plates of pasta smothered in delicious tomato soup, and Hot Pockets, leading me to suggest my wife make a habit of the Adderall. After devouring our fill, we laid ourselves down.

The children, in spite of the novelty of the hammocks, were quickly asleep. In vain I tried to follow their example; a thousand anxious thoughts presented themselves, and as quickly as I dispelled them, others arose in their place. How would we build our house? What would we do when the Hot Pockets ran out? Is it wrong to touch yourself when you hear farm animals mating? The night wore on, and I was still awake. The fire burned low, and I rose and replenished it with dry fuel. Then again I climbed into my hammock, and toward morning fell asleep.

CHAPTER 12

The Grass House

*"People in grass houses
shouldn't get stoned."*

Early the next morning we awoke and immediately gathered together for the first round of the Great Experiment—having forgotten about the joints Ernest rolled the day before just moments after rolling them. My wife distributed the five joints of Hydroponic.

Fritz had already begun work on a foundation for the first floor of our marijuana manse. Meanwhile, my wife and I shotgunned a hit between us as a gesture of love—the boys groaned in horror. After each joint had burned down to a nib, we began to relay our experiences while Jack played secretary. He wrote it all down in the captain's log, taking real care with his words and penmanship such that the importance of this task would not be lost on any who might stumble across it at some later time.

"Day One," he titled the log, *"Hydroponic,"* followed by each of our names and the way we described our sensation. For our first attempt at finding the very best high and a first-of-its-kind ranking system for marijuana, things went quite well. Only Ernest—beside whose name was written, *"Feels like a cross between a silly tree and a globinmaker,"* caused a debate about whether or not he might have meant *goblin*maker, which still didn't clear things up, not to mention caused a spelling complication that took us an hour and a half to sort out—gave us any doubt as to the scientific and meaningful way in which our family intended to undertake this matter.

Next we laid down the rules, agreeing that we would spend all day smoking only the Hydroponic so that we could record final thoughts before bed. We were each to keep track of how much we smoked and by what means. Then in turn we nominated a strain for the next day and drew from a hat. All of us were pleased when my wife pulled NYC Diesel. It would be a nice test to smoke city bud in a tree.

Five joints were quickly arranged on a table made of a wide bough, and when Ernest lit one and began to smoke it accidentally, forgetting the rules of the experiment and that it was not to be enjoyed until tomorrow—we all decided, to hell with it, and shared it with him, then decided to seek out Fritz to hide the other four so that the same mistake would not be repeated.

When we found Fritz, he had assembled a few layers of bricks on the ground to form a smooth solid floor. As he went he was using a large paintbrush and a cauldron of boiling black tar in order to waterproof each layer. Jack asked how he'd procured such a substance to which his brother replied that he had been scraping the resin out of every bowl and pipe in our possession ever since we had arrived on the island—deciding early on it could be made into an excellent compound for waterproofing.

Looking at the boiling cauldron, I asked simply, "Will that be enough?"

"There's more," he answered.

"More? You mean you have more than one cauldron full of the thin black film left on a bowl after the pot is smoked? How much more could you possibly have?"

With that the boy revealed a beach ball–size black orb of the sticky goo, which he had wisely packed in leaves.

"Wait," I went on, truly amazed, "since we've been on this island—what, a few days?"

"Four months," he added.

"Four months?"

He nodded. I looked at my wife, who shrugged unknowing.

"Okay . . . so in four months we made that much resin?" By this point we had smoked the four joints of NYC Diesel we'd meant to hide from ourselves.

"Well, actually . . ." and he revealed four more balls of equal size and a fifth he had begun rolling about the size of a coconut.

"Really?" I asked again.

"Have you met you guys?" he returned, turning his back and resuming his work.

Once he had the first row of bricks down and coated, he laid another and another, until the house was five feet off the ground. He then built five steps up for easy access to the platform. Over the top of the floor he laid a row of palm fronds as a fine carpeting and then around this platform he continued to pile up the fancy bricks two deep, leaving out several squares for windows over which he intended to use sailcloth as curtains and one arched entryway at the top of the stairs.

After imparting to Fritz the great results of our morning's experiment, we set about helping the architect and builder. Stacking the bricks using the sticky crystals and the compound our boy had developed from resin mixed with the sap of a nearby tree as sealant, our house was thus enclosed on three sides. The fourth wall was the giant tree trunk against which our home was built. The two aforementioned windows were left open to admit a fresh sea breeze blowing in directly.

Fritz then made the roof of the room by strengthening bamboo poles with magic and baling them together in rows of five, bundling each of these collections of four. Using them like lightweight logs, he laid them over top the first floor and cut them to fit, nailing them together with long spears of sharpened bamboo hammered down deep into the walls. He then placed a second layer running the other direction over top of the first for extra strength.

Fritz then began the assemblage of two upstairs bedrooms. He had calculated a well-endowed tree branch jutting overhead, offering the foundation for a solid roofing structure, and even though we all muttered, "It's fine, dude, enough already, this place's great," Fritz insisted we enclose it still further. He did so by tying together long palm fronds, coating them in his special sealant, and then leaving them to dry in the sun.

While the other boys and Elizabeth and I sat around enjoying those fumes, Fritz began hauling up our hammocks and bedding and slung them from the branch. A few hours of daylight still remaining, he then built the walls for the second floor of our pot-house—leaving space for additional windows and clearing the floor from leaves and chips, and then building a table out of whichever bricks remained along with a few benches. After working like slaves all day, Fritz and I flung ourselves on the grass, while my wife arranged supper on the table he had made.

"Come," said she at length, "come and taste the cheesy scramble, and tell me how you like it. Ernest assured me that it would be much better if I threw in some canned tomatoes we found among the snacks, and I have been following his directions."

Laughing at the idea of Ernest turning scientific cook, we sat down. The fowls gathered round us to pick up the crumbs, while Master Nips skipped about freaking us all out by chattering and mimicking our gestures continually.

After we ate, we looked up at what was certainly an architectural masterpiece. Fritz attached the palm-frond roof as we instructed carefully to move left, no right, then a little left again. Finally our home was complete.

"Come, it is getting late," I said. "We and the chickens must go to roost."

We left the dogs pretending like they were on guard below and climbed up the marijuana staircase Fritz had, at the last minute, also managed to construct, replacing the hanging rope-ladder my wife deemed too dangerous. Fritz, Ernest, Franz, and Jack took the steps by twos and were up in a moment.

Their mother followed very cautiously, for though she had originated the idea of building a home out of this field of weed, she hesitated to entrust herself to the handiwork of four stoners and a twenty-four-year-old born-again Rasta-man who had given up marijuana. However, when she was safely on the second floor of the house—essentially two rooms with a wall and curtained door between them—I decided it was safe enough and followed.

Then for the first time we stood all together in our new home. With a greater sense of security than I had enjoyed since we landed on the island, I was about to offer up our evening prayer taking the bowl to my lips—poised to light—when everyone gasped.

"No, Father! You mustn't!"

"Ah yes," I said laughing. "People in grass houses shouldn't get stoned."

With everyone laughing, we climbed into our hammocks and retired for the night.

CHAPTER 13

An Herb of Which Dreams Are Made

I told the children we could give up on our experiment and just smoke willy-nilly— in honor of the Sabbath.

The next morning we were all awake early. After smoking more of the NYC Diesel we added a joint each of Candy Graham, which we agreed unanimously made for a far more excited buzz than yesterday's Hydro/Diesel combo, as the children sprang about the tree like young monkeys.

"If only we'd known that when I began the house," Fritz cried. "You were no better than a pile of those stinky marijuana bricks I spent all that time stacking."

"All that time!" I replied. "But it was only a day!"

"No, Father—it was a week. It felt like four or five weeks. You all mostly slept and ate and rolled around like giant sloths, but it was most definitely six full days."

"Note that in the log, young Jack," I ordered.

"What shall we do today, Father?" they all shouted.

"Why, rest!" I replied.

"Rest?" they repeated. "We feel amazing. Why should we rest?"

"'Six days shalt thou labor and do all that thou hast to do, but on the seventh, thou shalt do no manner of work.' This is the seventh day," I replied, "on it, therefore, let us rest."

"Six minutes of labor is more like it!" mumbled Fritz kicking dirt, "How about *I'll* rest! How about *I* won't do any work. . . . Six days of work my a . . . ."

"That is not resting," I said interrupting his complaints, "that is not the way you should spend Jah's day."

"Fine, but there's no church here, and there is nothing to do."

"We can worship here regardless," I said.

"But there is no church, no clergyman, and no organ," added Franz, agreeing with his oldest brother.

"The leafy shade of these great plants is far more beautiful than any church," I said. "Here we will worship our creator. Come, boys, turn the downstairs room into a dining hall."

The children, one by one, slipped down the steps.

"My dear Elizabeth," I said, "this morning you and I will devote ourselves to the Lord in the best way of all, by means of a parable." And with that, my wife and I took a tumble in our hammock, consecrating our home and our new and great lives together.

My wife was wholly agreeable and amazingly hot. We ate a fine breakfast of Honey Nut Cheerios and coconut milk, and the family assembled around me, as we sat in the pleasant shade on the fresh, soft grass.

After singing some Marley and offering a small bowl of potent Lowryder to the Almighty Giver of All Good, I told the children we could give up on our experiment and just smoke willy-nilly—in honor of the Sabbath.

"Oh, that would be delightful! I like our experiments," said Franz. "But sometimes it hurts my head to think about how, when, where, and why I am toking. I'd much rather just smoke whatever I want wherever I want."

"Ah, my little boy, I know what you mean, but a little discipline in this regard will be good for all of us," I returned. "Finding the absolute perfect high will give all of us greater joy in the long run."

"And fewer headaches," my wise wife added.

We then took up a sensational drum circle that went on and on until Franz complained that his hands would bleed and Jack called him a total wuss and soon my wife and I had to split up a fight. Thus with a final bowl for Jah and a short prayer for a blessing on our new home, we brought the service to a close.

When we realized Fritz had already gone off, we each decided to do as we wanted and dispersed.

I smoked some AK-47 and made friends with the fairies under the moss bed.

Ernest came to beg me to make him a skirt out of dried palm and two coconut cups for a bikini top. I told him to go off and do it himself so that I too might be able to laugh at the surprise of such a costume. Meanwhile Fritz was busy doing something to his tiger skin that smelled awful unless you sat there for a while and then it began to smell a little bit like Colby cheese. Jack was making arrows out of bamboo and, using a quiver he had made out of bark and some of his mother's yarn, began shooting them into the sea.

As everyone was thus employed, we were all surprised at hearing a shot just overhead. At the same moment two small birds fell dead at our feet, and looking up, we saw Ernest leaning out of the window and crying, "OMG! What have I done?"

He disappeared into the house and soon came running out the front door, and picking up the birds, he began to weep over them. One was a kind of thrush and the other a small dove. Carefully extracting the gun from the hand of my miserable child, I warned him that next time the luck might be with the birds rather than with his beloved family.

The good news I contrived looking upon the dead specimens was that the figs on which these birds had come to feed were only just beginning to ripen. It was probable that they would soon flock in numbers to the tree above our pot-house, which meant our house was definitely going to be shit-covered if we didn't kill them in large quantities. Fritz added that we might provide ourselves with valuable food for the rainy season if we did so by cooking them with melted lard or butter poured over them.

We of course laughed at the notion since, come on, who's got time to do all that?

Ernest went off to bury the victims of his accidental massacre. Jack, on the other hand, had manufactured a good supply of arrows and had been industriously practicing his archery all day. The youthful hunter now replenished his collection of arrows and came toward the tree looking, as his mother said laughing, like an innocent little Cupid, bent on conquest. This made everyone hungry.

During dinner, the boys and I decided to name all the different spots we had visited on the island. For instance, we agreed it would be cumbersome to have to say, "the little island at the mouth of our bay, where we found the dead shark," or "the large stream near our tent, across from which we made the bridge," or "that wood where we found coconuts, and caught the monkey," and so on.

As we decided upon the name for the bay in which we had landed, the conversation went like this:

"Let's call it Oyster Bay," suggested Fritz.

"How about Lobster Bay," said Jack, "in memory of the old fellow who grabbed onto my nose? Wait . . . was that me?"

"No, no!—Avatar," I countered, "because seriously, how cool."

"I think," observed my great wife, "that, as a token of gratitude for our escape, we should call it Safety Bay."

This name met with several utterances of "Meh," but more of a general disinterest and therefore agreement.

Other names were quickly chosen. Our first place of abode we called Hot Pocket Freedom Tent. It was a combination of *Hot Pocket* in honor of the painfully hot setting we endured there and a name we were likely to remember, and *freedom* because it was the place that brought us our first taste of true marijuana-loving freedom. The islet in the bay became Rubber Bracelet for no reason, and the reedy swamp was Skunk 1, because it smelled like it. It was some time before the serious question of a name for our leafy castle could be decided. But finally it was titled Dankhurst after the great and perfect buzz it represented. Then we rapidly named the few remaining points: Blueberry Hill, the height we first ascended; Cape Ditchweed from whose rocky heights we had looked in vain for our ship's crew; and Strawberry Field Forever because several people wanted to call it Blueberry Hill also and we needed a good compromise. This concluded our geographical nomenclature.

In the afternoon the boys went on with their various activities. Fritz finished working on his tiger skin and hung it on the downstairs wall for decoration, having accomplished a truly impressive likeness of young Elvis on the front. Jack shot the rest of his arrows, and then set to making more out of porcupine quills, which concerned all of us.

I spent some time discussing with Turk his ideas about full body armor manufactured for dogs. He then showed me how to wrap him in coconut shells with nails pounded through. Once dressed, the animal could easily fight the fiercest beast he might encounter, while protected by armor that was both defensive and offensive. Even Juno refused to go near him. I shook off the idea that this creature that lacked opposable thumbs might have somehow used me.

Amid these interesting occupations the evening drew on, and after a pleasant walk through the sweet glades near our abode, we closed our Sabbath day with the six-footer and a go-around with the hookah, retiring to rest with peaceful hearts.

The next morning, I proposed an expedition to Hot Pocket Freedom Tent, saying I wished to make my way there by a different route. We left Dankhurst well armed— I, and two of my sons, carrying a gun and game-bag, while Jack was equipped with his bow and quiver full of arrows. We thought it best to keep explosives and firearms from Ernest all together.

Elizabeth and I walked together, she, of the whole party, being the only other person unarmed by choice, carried a jar in which to get butter from Hot Pocket Freedom Tent. We were preceded by the dogs—Turk was scaring the pants off everybody with his stunning armor including Juno who kept at a respectful distance from her formidable companion.

Master Nips had fully intended to mount him for a ride but when he saw him in his sharp new skin, he approached him carefully, and touching him with one paw, discovered that such a hide would make anything but an agreeable seat. His comical grimace made all of us laugh as he bounded toward Juno, jumping up on her back and seating himself there instead.

An odd flamingo came with us, too, for some time keeping beside the children, following first one, then another as they explored the dense fields of flowering cannabis on either side. The boys' irregular steps soon disgusted the flamingo, and so he came to walk sedately by my side as I shared a fine spliff with my wife and spoke to the bird who called himself Thelma and told me that the Reno library was really a lovely place for an afternoon nap.

We strolled on in the cool afternoon air, following the stream. The boys roamed ahead, intent on exploration.

Suddenly there was a joyful shout, and I saw Ernest and Jack running at full speed toward me. In the younger boy's hand, he held a plant, and, panting for breath, and with sparkling eyes, he held it up to me.

"Magic Kush, Father," he gasped.

"My dear Jack," I said, taking the multihued treasure from the boy and holding it closer to smell the unmistakable aroma of autumn, apple pie, and a hint of fifth-grade classroom, for there was no mistaking the flower and leaf, and the bright red crystals climbing up all sides of the stem. "You have indeed made a discovery—but can we claim it is the very Magic Kush of which so many of us have dreamt? Might we really jump to that conclusion?"

"But come and look at it," Jack added. "While there is only a small patch of these stems, they are hardy."

We hurried to the spot and there, a small tract of ground was indeed covered with the precious plant.

"It would have been rather difficult," remarked Franz, "to have discovered such a great treasure were it not for Ernest's remarkable gift for tracking dank strains of cannabis."

"Very true," agreed Fritz, smiling, "but Ernest so often mistakes things—I'm surprised he didn't tell us he'd discovered a potato field!"

"True," agreed Jack laughing, until everyone joined in on the peals of laughter, including good-hearted Ernest who had by now dug up, with hands and knife, one of the plants to harvest. So delighted were we with the discovery, and so eager to possess it, until Fritz pointed out the meager quantity and encouraged us to use prudence in our actions until we could plant additional seeds to supply ourselves with more.

Magic Kush was a near-mythologized strain of marijuana. None of us had ever even seen it with our own eyes. The promise was of a high so perfect that the universe immediately met with the spirit of he who smoked it in perfect alignment. It turned angry men kind and kind men saintly. So valuable a commodity was the Magic Kush that we immediately stopped digging it up.

Some wished to return at once to Dankhurst to burn and taste our new acquisition; but this I overruled, for it would have to be at a ceremony of great importance. I expected to look upon it as a special treat to be enjoyed with great care and respect. Asking Fritz to mark and keep the location of the special plants, we continued our march with but the single harvested stem dug up by Ernest safely in my bag and the bud he had pulled off in his pocket.

"How," I wondered, "can we thank the giver of all these blessings, sufficiently?"

"We can get naked and act out the fourth hour of *Fanny and Alexander*," offered Ernest.

"Or," said Franz, "we can say, 'We thank thee, Great Jah, for your goodness and mercy—and bless us for Yeshu's sake. Toke. Toke. Toke. Amen.'"

"That isn't enough," said Fritz. "We must show with great love and respect that although this island is abundant in all Jah's greatest gifts, we cannot just partake of them like gluttonous monsters. We cannot pull them up and suck them down as though they are an expendable commodity."

And as he said it, both Franz and Ernest lit up joints. My oldest son looked with disappointment upon the younger men.

"You are quite right, Fritz," I agreed. "However, Franz and Ernest are not *you* and must praise Jah in their own way."

"But if all you do is smoke and eat and take from this great island that has done more than rescue and deliver us, but is Eden itself, how do you know you will go on giving value to the great gifts it bestows?"

"How do you suppose we do this?" I asked, jonesing for a hit of the joints being freely passed among the other members of my family, but also accounting for the powerful speech of my son.

"Just pay attention, Father," the boy cautioned. "There is money yet to be made."

His formidable warning made my hair stand on end. Then we reached the head of our stream where it fell from the rocks in a beautiful, sparkling, splashing cascade. We crossed and entered even more strains of tall, beautiful, crystal-covered grasses on the other side.

We forced our way through with difficulty, so thick and tangled were the stems. The landscape was lovely. Rich tropical vegetation flourished on every side—tall stately palms surrounded by luxuriant ferns, brilliant flowers, and graceful creepers, the prickly cactus shooting up among them, along with aloe, jasmine, and sweet-scented vanilla—the thriving strains of marijuana interwoven throughout were enough to make any man fall to his knees in praise of Jah—there was ripe Indica, while regal Skunk Red Hair loaded the breath of the evening breeze with her rich perfume. The boys were delighted with the strains of Durban Poison, and so eagerly did they begin to harvest it and gnaw its leaves that my wife had to caution them that there were no doctors on our island, and that if they became ill, they would have to cure themselves or face the "butter cure" she swore by.

This advice, however, seemed to have little effect on my sons, and showing Nips the monkey what they wanted, they sent him after the plants farthest from their grasp.

While my family was entertained, Fritz and I examined the other shrubs and bushes. Among these I noticed one that I knew well from description to be the Supernova.

"Come here, boys," I said, "here is something of far more value than your Skunk Red Hair. Do you see that plant with long pointed leaves and beautiful sticky crystals? That is the Supernova. The filaments of the leaves make delicious teas, while the leaves themselves can be used to form an invaluable ameliorant that soothes ailments from nausea to the common cold. And the pith of this wonderful plant may be woven into useful cloths and strong fabrics."

When I saw how right Fritz was when he said that none of the boys any longer valued and respected this incredible place onto which we had been deposited, I decided a lesson was in order.

"Suppose, Jack, you had been wrecked here, how would you have made a fire without matches or lighters?"

"As the savages do," he replied, "I would rub two pieces of wood together until they lit."

"Try it," I said. "For the next twenty-four hours, I will be taking from each of you your matches and lighters. You may have all the cannabis you desire, but you will not be able to light it afire with anything but your ingenuity."

The boys were, at first, delighted with the experiment and eagerly gave up their lighting implements to my care.

"We'll see how long their excitement lasts," smirked Fritz.

"Wait until you see the creative lengths a man will go to in order to make it to his drug," advised his mother.

"I'd watch out for your safety, Father," Fritz warned, alarming me enough so that when no was looking, I buried the lighting implements and only showed the burial location to my eldest so that he might remind me where I had done so twenty-four hours later.

Master Jack was already off and rubbing stones together, while young Franz was having some success with a small pile of dry pine needles and a magnifying glass. Ernest was otherwise occupied with his arms wrapped tightly around a fig tree, hugging it importantly and calling it Sonny.

I had to interrupt everyone to continue our march. At length, we reached Hot Pocket Freedom Tent where everything was safe, and we set to work to collecting what we wanted. I opened the butter cask from which my wife could take her fill, watching with some alarm as she rubbed it across her face and neck. Fritz gathered ammunition, being the only one sober enough to remain cautious of our unknown environs. Jack and Ernest ran races to and from the beach against fowl and canine.

Finally Fritz reminded us to gather up the fowl, some salt, and a few additional crates of harvested doobage for the road. As the group was steadily sobering up without the usual tools for fire making, we actually succeeded in organizing for our needs quite well. After a cheerful and pleasant walk, we once more reached our weedy abode. Then, following a delicious supper of potatoes out of a box mixed with butter, Ernest, who was as clear-eyed as I had ever seen him, remarked that the great deal of driftwood on the beach would make an excellent sled to pull goods from Hot Pocket Freedom Tent to Dankhurst.

I awoke early and enlisted Ernest to be my assistant, wishing to encourage him to try out a morning of sobriety. After a little stretching and yawning, he got up, and while his agitation was palpable, he followed me to the beach in silence. I agreed to bring along the donkey to carry our load.

As we went along, I remarked to Ernest that feeling sorry for himself about a single day without fire on an island such as this was hardly productive. I advised he spend this walk thinking of useful ways out of his predicament. I even made him watch as I myself smoked an entire bowl with a handy lighter in front of his lustful eyes.

"Oh, Father, do not accuse me of laziness! Indeed I mean to figure out a way to make fire. I am fine going with you to get wood with which to make a sled. But I had intended to use this morning to rub sticks together as hard and long as I could, and I know there will be plenty of time afterward. But whatever you just smoked smelled so good. And the other boys will be well ahead of me and I imagine they will have greater luck than I."

"Well, Ernest, I think that showing a little appreciation for what you have in the moments when you don't have it is often the time a man is strongest."

"How would you know? You just smoked a huge bowl of Purple Haze."

"Ah yes, but before this day, I had many more days than you running from the fuzz, or smoking my doobie in basements until I taught myself to play guitar so I could become a rock star and freely get stoned in the back rooms of rock clubs. So now, as I pull on all this excellent, abundant bud, alone on this great island except for the people I love most, I am truly grateful, my son. And I worry, the way I have seen you smoking until you are unable to recognize human from Hot Pocket, that you do not have the same appreciation."

Ernest and I went along in silence the rest of the way. I hoped it was because of my speech, although it may also have been that I was so blitzed out, I forgot to answer any subsequent questions.

Once we were on the seashore, our work was quickly accomplished. Ernest selected the wood, and the donkey dragged it homeward, along with a small chest I unearthed while I was building a sand sculpture of a mermaid nearby.

We heard the boys grinding rocks and sticks together and generally yelling and cursing at each other. They ran to meet us, nearly crying, their pleading for a match or a lighter was so great. I distracted them by presenting the chest to them and suggesting it might be filled with jewels.

The chest only contained a whistle, a phone charger, and a Disney Princess's T-shirt soaked by seawater.

Ernest gave us a fashion show with the T-shirt during breakfast, after which we discussed the various failures that had thwarted all of my sons' attempts to make fire. They decided instead to work together, noting that practice would ultimately make them perfect. Entirely agreeing with their view on the subject, I encouraged them to work hard until they accomplished their goal.

While they were busily at work, Fritz and I got started on the sled. But first I decided to test out a super-cool vaporizer I had discovered back at Hot Pocket Freedom Tent while Fritz was wrapping the driftwood with large strips of bark. I soon found myself inside the curved front stanchion of the completed sled, enjoying myself as my boy pulled me around camp pretending I was a cask of butter or as good as, he said.

When we went to show the boys what we'd done, they were harried and sallow-faced. Even Jack who was usually up for any adventure seemed edgy and discontented. No doubt they had been discussing this hardship, for little Franz came to me with a brilliant proposal of his own.

"Papa," said he, "what if we used a little gunpowder? I mean, that would have to lead to fire, wouldn't it? And you never said we couldn't use any means at our disposal."

I burst into a roar of laughter, which probably wasn't so very nice of me given the ongoing struggle of the little fellow.

"Come, Fritz," I said, "tell your brother what gunpowder really is."

"Gunpowder is made of charcoal, sulfur, and saltpeter mixed together, and if you try to light a joint with it, you'll probably kill yourself or one of those two."

My wife meanwhile was no longer enjoying the frustration of most of her children. "Give them back their tools," she begged on their behalf, "or I shall give them mine."

"Good wife," I promised, "if they have not come up with fire for themselves by then, I will replace their apparatuses as soon as we have eaten dinner."

But just then, a roar of happiness erupted as when I looked back, a small fire was working itself up on the ground.

"It was my fart!" Jack exclaimed. "I felt it coming on—and I knew that the flint was sparking just enough to ignite it—so I sat on a pile of twigs and dried leaves, sparked the stone, and, ta-da! Fire!"

Each boy was now holding his own panatella cigarette in two hands. Fritz stayed behind with his mother as the rest of us made our way back toward Hot Pocket Freedom Tent to find the place I had stashed all the matches and lighters. We were all also interested in the patch of Magic Kush.

We harnessed both cow and donkey to the sled and, accompanied by Juno, cheerfully departed, going back the way we had gone before. Except somehow we ended up at Hot Pocket Freedom Tent without coming across the place I had left our fire-starting tools or the special pot patch.

Accepting that we would find it on our way back, we began to load the sled, not only with the butter-barrel, but with the gunpowder, a crate of Velveeta, and a variety of other items—a hookah, a basketball, a B. A. Baracus action figure, some tools, a game of Battleship, a dog-eared copy of *Valley of the Dolls*, and Turk's armor, which Juno tricked me into taking after intentionally leaving it behind the first time.

Upon making our way back to Dankhurst, we agreed it had probably not been in our best interests to have tested out the hookah because soon we were among a series of bold and precipitous cliffs, which extended into the deep water and rose abruptly, forming an inaccessible wall of rocks. Here the ground was swampy and overgrown with large tangled plants.

It was quite some time before we got Franz out of them, figured out our bearings by way of the shore, and were able to carry on. Jack pointed out that Ernest was missing, but there wasn't much we could do about it. We yelled out to him but to no avail. Then we heard, "Father!" and "Jack! Franz!"

Hastening toward the spot, we saw the boy lying in the grass, a fatty skinned up and one lighter in each of his hands lighting the end.

"This is wonderful, Ernest!" I cried. "You have found the hidden stash of lighters and matches." Admittedly I was extra relieved because I myself was down to my last lighter, having lost track of any other paraphernalia with which I had started. I made a mental note I then immediately forgot, to collect all paraphernalia off the ship to store someplace safe along with the musical instruments.

We did one last giant sweep of the area looking for the precious Magic Kush before we got caught up in a game of mango baseball and it got late and became time to continue the journey home.

We kept inland and were skirting the borders of a grassy thicket, when Juno suddenly plunged into the bushes. Moments later, the single, most bizarre-looking creature I ever beheld jumped out. It was taking enormous flying leaps and landing in a sitting posture, moving over the ground at an astonishing rate. I attempted to shoot it as it passed, but missed.

Chasing it, we all followed it into a giant hole and found ourselves falling fast. As we fell, our hands and feet seemed to grow and shrink until at last we found ourselves standing at the bottom of the ocean with the beast before us, still and creepy.

It was as large as a cow, and its head was shaped like that of a mouse. Its skin was the color of a fawn. It had long ears like a hare and a tail like a tiger's. The forepaws resembled those of a squirrel, but they seemed only half-grown while the hind legs were enormous, and so long, that when upright the animal looked as if it was on stilts.

For some time, we stood silently staring at the remarkable creature before us. I could not recollect having ever seen or heard of anything like it.

"Well, Father," the creature said in Ernest's voice, "I should say this is about the strangest beast anywhere."

"Hello, sir," I said, not in the least surprised to hear myself speak underwater, "I cannot think what animal you are. May I examine your teeth?"

The creature nodded and Jack took the pleasure. "I see four sharp incisor teeth, Father—two upper, and two under, like a squirrel."

"Ah! Then he is a rodent. What rodents can you remember, Franz?"

"I don't know, the mouse, the marmot, the squirrel, the hare, the beaver, the jerboa—"

"The jerboa!" I exclaimed. "Another imaginary species… The jerboa! You, sir, are very much like a jerboa, only larger. You must be a kangaroo, one of the animals that has a pouch for its young. You were discovered by the great Captain Cook, and I congratulate you on being the first specimen in Stonerland!" I said, laughing, as I named our island.

The kangaroo was added to the already heavy load on our sled, and we proceeded slowly, up from the bottom of the ocean to arrive late at Dankhurst. We were met with the usual bright welcome. Fritz and Elizabeth were confused by our story, especially the part about falling down a rabbit hole to the bottom of the ocean—and the stowaway himself hopped off the sled without so much as a hello to the rest of the family.

Fritz alone wore an expression of dissatisfaction, and I could see that he was struggling against his jealous feelings, that he had not been there when we had gone to a magic place underwater. I wondered momentarily if his sobriety wouldn't ultimately distance him so much from the rest of his family that it might ultimately tear us apart. Then I put a lady's tutu on Nips from one of the chests we'd brought back and clapped while he turned in circles.

"What a great day!" Ernest said. And all but one agreed.

As the shades of night approached, we concluded the day's work by preparing a dinner of Hot Pockets and beer. The animals were fed, and our own supper was eaten with great appetite. We smoked a large and well-deserved spliff and retired, with thankful hearts, to sound and well-earned sleep.

CHAPTER 14

My Son Finds a Mate . . . I Mean, a Man

. . . we would not be as easily taken.
We would get them really, really high
and then force-feed them Twinkies so
they would grow to love us.

The next morning, while preparing breakfast, I called Ernest and Jack to instruct them in the next steps for our ongoing experiment. We were sorely in need of a method by which we could keep everything organized. We required a way to store and separate each strain of ganja to maintain an honest record of their properties. It would further prove important for harvesting down the road to keep our stash clearly marked. Since organization was not our strong suit, I enlisted Fritz to help.

He, however, had disappeared directly after breakfast, and his mother could only guess that, since we needed potatoes, and a field of them had been recently discovered near a second field of greens, cucumber, cabbage, and radishes provided by Jah, he might have gone to fetch a supply. I left my dear wife alone with little Franz and took Jack and Ernest with me back to the wreck. I intended to bring back jars, crates, musical instruments, and additional storage containers, along with a Sharpie and a labeler to play with.

Advancing steadily on our way, we passed under the bridge over Strawberry Fields Forever, which was a river and not a field and was confusing for us. The current carried us briskly out of the bay. We were very soon moored however unsafely alongside the wreck, and scrambling up her shattered sides, we stood on what remained of the deck and began at once to lay our plans. I wanted to make a raft to carry a great variety of articles too large and heavy for our present boat.

A number of empty water-casks seemed just what was required for the raft's foundation. I did not accompany the boys when they went to sit in the crow's nest for an afternoon toke. Instead I arranged the barrels side by side in four rows of three; too burned out to figure in exact numbers, I ended up with between eight and fifteen barrels. I secured them with two wood flats atop and soon had a first-rate raft (or second-rate, depending on whether you were looking at it from the port or starboard side), suited to our purpose. When the boys returned, they were so shocked to see what I'd accomplished they needed to sit down for a moment and hear me tell it in narrative form. I added a fairy queen and a pair of bickering conjoined twin brothers for comic relief to keep their attention. When they believed me that I'd actually built the raft and not been gifted it by an evil sea monster, they skinned me up a rolly.

It would have been impossible to return to land that evening, for we were thoroughly fatigued by my labors.

We made an excellent supper from the ship's provisions, including the Hostess Pantry and an ingenious burrito of corn tortillas rolled up with salami, Nutella, and Grey Poupon, which we all found alarmingly delicious after packing up enough Baby Bhang to annihilate a small village. Then resting for the night on spring mattresses, a perfect luxury to us, after our narrow hammocks, we fell asleep.

The next morning we loaded the raft and boat with jars, crates, tins, and the thousands of Ziploc Baggies we found on board. Jack discovered a stash of airtight jars numbering easily into the hundreds. They appeared large enough to hold a substantial harvest, not that spatial relations were a strong suit. Ernest stumbled upon a labeler—or Jack and

I stumbled on Ernest in the captain's quarters covered in small labels that said things like, "Ultra QT," "Table 4 2," and "Sxy Grlfrnd."

The future organization of our pot stash now under control, we took a few chairs and a few doors and window frames, with their bolts, bars, and locks as a special gift for Fritz—and also because we were paranoid. We emptied the feathers from each mattress to bring back the outer casing because we each thought we had a better idea for what we would stuff them with. Mine was sweet smelling and crystal-covered. Jack's was fluffy and green and schwaggish. Ernest's was imaginary and included the hair of the gibbon and powdered unicorn horn.

One large chest was filled with an assortment of sparkly things at which none of us could stop staring. It reminded us of a jeweler's shop, so glittering was the display of gold and silver watches, snuffboxes, buckles, studs, chains, rings, and all manner of trinkets. These we took because, at least according to Ernest, the belt buckle was itself an antenna that could be linked to an orbiting satellite that allowed him to channel Showtime's *The Tudors* and *The L Word* as well as the 1945 Berlin Olympics—at least, the track and field events.

The cargo, which had been meant to take our family and the crew to a private stoner island, proved in fact a rich and almost inexhaustible treasure to us. We gathered up bongs, screens, pipes, Ho Hos, porn, spray paint, and all that was necessary for the fulfillment and care of hardcore stoners. There were lighters, matches, bongos, two kiddie-pianos, a whole box of harmonicas and maracas, and one colorful xylophone.

So bewildered were we by the wealth around us that for some time we were at a loss as to what else to remove to the raft and just stood staring and drooling a little. It would be impossible to take everything, yet any storm would completely destroy the ship, and we would lose the rest.

Selecting a number of the most useful articles, however, including of course the hookahs with the sparkliest decoration, and a very cool collection of international coins, we filled the raft, leaving behind unnecessary items like fruit trees, huge bags of cement, other building materials, and any tools that could be used in tanning leather, preserving food, or sewing, since we wouldn't know how to use it anyway. On the other hand, we were really proud of ourselves for remembering to bring everything from the Hostess pantry, potting soils, harvesting tools, musical instruments, rolling papers, and a very nice pair of pink gloves . . . for my wife.

Early in the afternoon, both of our craft were heavy with supplies, and we were ready to go. The sea was calm and the wind was steady. We found we could spread the sail, and make good progress. Jack asked me for the telescope, as he had observed something floating in the water. Then handing it back, he asked if we could see what it was. It turned out to be a sleeping turtle.

"Steer toward it!" he exclaimed. I did so with my mind, so that he might have a better look at the creature. Little did I suspect what he intended to do. With his back turned to Ernest and me, and the sail blocking my view, all of a sudden, I experienced a shock, as suddenly the little boat bolted forward and was rapidly drawn through the water.

"Jack, what are you doing?" we cried. "You are sending us to the bottom of the sea."

"I have him, hurrah! I have him safe!" he shouted back in eager excitement. "Or not so safe!" he added as we lurched forward and took on some water. However, to my amazement, once we leveled out, I saw that he had thrown a rope about the animal's body so that it was easily pulling us through the water.

"For heaven's sake, be careful! The instant there is danger, cut the line!"

The turtle began to make for the open sea. At this point Ernest fell back and accidentally hoisted the sail, which happily made us too heavy for it to pull in that direction. The creature directed its course landward, drawing us rapidly after it. The part of the shore to which the turtle was heading was to the left of our usual landing-place. The beach there shelved very gradually, and at some distance from land we grounded with a sharp jolt but fortunately without capsizing.

The turtle was evidently greatly exhausted, and no wonder, since it had been acting as a tug boat, and had been dragging, at full speed, a couple of heavily laden vessels and three stoners. Its intention was to escape to land; but I leaped into the water, and wading up to it, cut it free.

Ernest thanked the turtle for his help and tried to kiss it, but Jack pulled him away before he accomplished this act of animal cruelty. As we were by no means far from

Dankhurst, Elizabeth and Franz appeared in the distance running eagerly toward us and our new prizes.

Anxious to remove some of our goods before night, the boys ran off to fetch the sled and got lost and distracted for long enough that my wife and I could do it at least twice.

We then made our way home, smoking heavily and chatting merrily about our various adventures. It wasn't long before someone noticed an important item was missing—Fritz.

"Excuse me, but where is our brother?" asked little Franz.

Ernest, Jack, and I looked from one to the other. Was it possible he had been with us? Had we left him back at the wreck? After some debate:

Jack: "I don't think he was ever with us."

Me: "But I remember him eating an apple in the Hostess pantry."

Ernest: "Even for a liberal lesbian couple, Bette and Tina were still too self-involved to start a family in the first season."

My wife, ignoring Ernest, added, "He wasn't here yesterday when we awoke. Remember?"

Everyone nodded slowly, unsure if they were simply nodding to be part of the group, or nodding because they remembered.

My wife and Franz, though startled by the unexpected absence of Fritz, were still delighted that the rest of us had returned safely, and listened to our maritime adventures. My wife laughed with delight as she heard of our encounter with the turtle.

For dinner we ate some mac and cheese and chicken nuggets in the shape of aquatic animals about whose origins no one asked, but which both Elizabeth and Franz looked upon with sheepish pride. We smoked heavily and went to sleep.

Five days passed and Fritz still remained absent. I was nervous, and at last decided to go look for him. Everyone thought this a good idea, especially my wife who mumbled, "It only took you five days to get around to it."

I got into the boat that bright morning and with a favorable breeze, took all five of us for a pleasant ride to find my missing son.

Our little yacht bounded over the water happily, and the bright sunshine and delicious sea breeze put us all in the highest spirits—even though we might have been headed off to retrieve a corpse, we had smoked enough Bobo Bush that we kept forgetting and had to ask each other repeatedly, "Where are we going? Oh, yeah."

Soon, straight ahead, I saw a dark and shadowy mass just below the surface of the water.

"A sunken rock," I thought to myself.

I tried to avoid it, but a catastrophe seemed inevitable. We surged ahead! A slight shock and all was over! The danger was passed!

I glanced over to look at it again but the rock was gone, and, where but a moment before I had distinctly seen its great green shadow, I now saw nothing.

Before we had recovered from our amazement, Jack surprised me with a shout.

"There is another rock," he exclaimed, "to starboard, Father!" Sure enough, there lay, apparently, another sunken rock.

"The rock is moving!" shouted Franz and at first I was surprised it hadn't been Ernest saying it was a moving rock and talking to it and trying to kiss it on the mouth, but sure enough a great black body emerged from the sea. With a mighty noise it rose upward, and then water fell like rain all around. Thus the mystery was explained—it was a whale.

Fearful stories occurred to me of the savage temper of whales, how they had been known to destroy boat after boat, and even to sink great ships, so with a feeling of desperation I smoked a little more reefer to calm my nerves. Jack led us in a chorus of "Kumbaya" until the good whale plunged beneath its surface and disappeared.

We kept a sharp lookout for him, but, as my wife pointed out, our singing wasn't pretty. We had probably scared it off.

The boys were about to cry out in victory, but just then, darting behind a rock they spied a canoe paddled by a tall and muscular savage, who now stood up in his skiff and appeared to be examining us attentively. Seeing that we were moving toward him, the swarthy native paddled behind a rock. An awful thought now took possession of me. There must be a tribe of these natives lurking on these shores, and Fritz must have fallen into their hands.

However, I was determined that we would not be as easily taken. We would get them really, really high and then force-feed them Twinkies so that they would grow to love us.

Presently another face appeared, peering at us from a rock up on the cliff. It vanished, and we saw another peering at us from lower down.

"Hoist a white flag," my wife said.

"We don't have one," we answered.

"Talk to them," she urged.

Ernest then, in perfect Malay which no one knew he spoke, called out, "*Natatae ako.*"

Jack hereupon lost patience and yelled, "Come here, you son of a gun, come onboard and make friends, or we'll blow you and your—"

"Stop! Stop! You foolish boy," I interjected. "You will alarm the man, with your wild words and gestures."

"No! But see," he replied, "he is paddling toward us!"

And sure enough the canoe was rapidly approaching.

A cry from Franz alarmed me. "Look! Look!" he shrieked. "The villain is wearing a wig made from Fritz's hair."

Ernest alone remained unmoved. He yelled out, waving peacefully, "Hey, Fritz! How's it going?"

The words were scarcely out of his mouth when I, too, recognized the well-known face.

In another minute the brave boy was on board and was kissed and heartily welcomed. He was assailed with a storm of questions from all sides—Where had he been? What had kept him so long? What was his opinion on interracial adoption (from Ernest, of course)?

"The last question," he replied with a smile, "is the only one I will answer now—the others shall be explained when I tell you all about my adventures.

"I think that as long as you are prepared to expose the child to his or her birth culture, race, and nationality—if applicable—there is no need to limit yourself when adopting a child, especially since adoption is, by itself, such a difficult undertaking for couples who want children."

We then described to him our adventure with the whale.

Then we all just looked at each other blankly for a minute until Fritz said, "I can lead you to an island where you can anchor. It is well worth seeing, for it contains all sorts of strange things." He then jumped back into his canoe and piloted us to a picturesque little island in the bay. We dropped our anchor and sprang ashore, following Fritz in perfect silence.

When we emerged from a thicket, we saw before us a hut built out of tree boughs, at whose entrance burned a cheerful fire.

Fritz scurried inside, leaving us mute with astonishment. In another moment he emerged, leading by the hand a handsome boy dressed like an English naval officer. The pair advanced to meet us, and Fritz, radiant with joy, introduced his companion as Edward Montrose.

"And," he continued, looking at his mother and me, "you will welcome him as a friend and a brother to our family circle."

"That we will, indeed!" my wife exclaimed with total equanimity, advancing and holding out her arms to take the fair young stranger into an embrace. "Our wild life may have roughened our looks and manners, but it has not hardened our hearts, I trust," she said.

I was silent, unsure whether I was simply stunned mute by the fact that there was another stowaway on our island or alarmed by the fact that it looked like my son was either gay or just horny enough to fall for anyone-not-related-by-blood, or perhaps I was just too high to talk.

Luckily my other boys immediately expressed their gratification at the appearance of a new friend. From Fritz's expressions it seemed that he was quite taken with the young man. And so I, too, smiled as warmly as I could and embraced the boy into our clan.

The young men then ran down to the boat to bring up a few provisions for supper, as well as to make preparations for a camp in which we would spend the night. This done, my wife set before us a substantial processed meal, while the boys, anxious to make their new acquaintance feel at home among them, were doing their best to amuse him. After the first feeling of strangeness had worn off, he entered fully into all their fun except, for the moment, he denied our offer of a toke explaining that he wanted to keep his wits about him. But by the time we sat down to supper everyone was laughing and chatting as gaily (no pun intended) as if he were as high as the rest of us—except Fritz. The young man enjoyed the food and mead and, without alluding once to his previous life, kept up a lively conversation.

The mere fact of meeting with any human being after so many weeks of isolation was in itself exciting. But that this person should be so handsome, so gay, and so perfectly charming seemed completely to have turned every single one of my boys into a flaming homosexual—not that there was anything wrong with that. When the feast ended, and their new friend was led to his sleeping bag, the rest of us toasted to the health of Edward Montrose and drank the fragrant mead, amid the cheers and clapping of hands.

When the boy was gone, and silence had been restored, Jack exclaimed:

"Fritz, just tell us where you came across this hot . . . I mean, *cool* dude. Did you go off looking for him, or did you meet him by chance?"

Jack threw more wood upon the blazing fire, and throwing himself down on the ground and lighting up a J, prepared to listen attentively.

Fritz, after a moment of hesitation, began, "I found a note in the water. 'Help the English castaway,' it said. So I decided to set out to find the sender. I told you guys. Don't you remember?"

We all shrugged. Maybe he had, maybe he hadn't. Who knew. . . .

He went on. "I built a kayak for two out of a hollowed-out tree. Then, with a hopeful heart I left you all and made for the open sea. For several hours I paddled steadily, the wind helping me as I glided. I kept near shore so should a storm arise, I might find some shelter.

"It was a good thing I did because I reached a protective cove just when that insane storm came up, remember that one? Boy, that was a doozy."

We froze, hoping the question was rhetorical. Luckily he went swiftly on with his tale.

"That storm turned the sea into one giant mess of foam with great surging waves and, even in the comparative calm of the bay, I still felt that I might be in danger.

"I slept that night in my kayak and the next morning, I went on. The wind had subsided and the sea was smooth. I looked in every direction to detect, if possible, the slightest trace of smoke, or other sign of human life. I paddled on till noon.

"The coast now began to change—the shores were sandy, while further inland lay dense forests, from whose gloomy depths I could hear the fierce roar of animals of prey, apes, hyenas, deer. I have never felt as lonely as I did while listening to the strange sounds of the island, and knowing that I was the only human being nearby.

"For some hours I paddled on, sometimes passing the mouth of a stream, sometimes that of a broad river. Had I been merely on an exploring expedition, I would have been tempted to cruise a little way up one of these pathways into the forest, but as I was otherwise occupied, such an idea did not enter my head. On, on, on, I felt I must go, until I reached the goal of my voyage.

"The night drew on and finding a sheltered cove, I anchored my kayak and stepped on shore. You know how good it felt to stretch my legs, after sitting for so long in the cramped position forced by the craft.

"Afraid to sleep onshore, I prepared a small supper of fish and seaweed; then I returned to my boat to spend the night.

"The next morning I landed again to eat breakfast. I lit a fire, and cooked a parrot I'd shot down from a tree. As it was cooking, I heard a rustle in the grass behind me. I glanced and there, with glaring eyes was an immense tiger.

"In another moment I would have been dinner, and our young guest would have been doomed to Jah only knows how many more years of solitude!

"My gun was at my side. I seized it and fired—and the animal, pierced through the heart, rolled over dead at my feet.

"I returned to my kayak, and leaving the great tiger lying where he fell, paddled hastily away.

"My thoughts were gloomy. I wondered if the stranger who'd written had done so from a different shore entirely. Every stroke of my paddle took me farther from people and safety—" Fritz looked from me to Ernest then back to me and amended—"well, from people. This feeling of loneliness did not last long for soon a sight presented itself, which banished all my doubts and fears, and elevated my spirits.

"A high hill crested before me. I rounded it, and found a calm and pleasant bay. In the distance rose a column of smoke, steadily and clearly curling upward in the calm air. I could scarcely believe my senses, and gazed at it, as though I were in a dream. Then, with a throbbing pulse and a giddy brain, I grabbed my paddle, and strained every nerve to reach it."

"Reach what?" interrupted Ernest.

"The smoke," answered his mother silencing him when he asked if he could have some.

Fritz went on, "A few strokes carried me across the bay, and, securing my canoe, I leaped upon the rock, on which the beacon was blazing. There was, however, no sign of a human being anywhere. I was about to shout, for the fire had recently been tended. I knew the stranger was not far off. But, before I could call out, I saw a figure passing along the chain of rocks toward me. You can all imagine my euphoria.

"I called out in Spanish: 'Pasar el jabon.'

Then, remembering that I was on the search for an *Englishman* I amended it to, "Welcome, fair stranger! Jah has heard your call, and has sent me to your aid!"

"Mr. Montrose came quickly forward and grasped my hands warmly, and said, 'Long, long, have I waited for someone to find me on this island. Thank you for coming—and who is Jah?'"

My boys were now excited by the news that our strange guest had never heard of the great Jah and made a fuss about it. Fritz explained that the young man was military and probably had better things to do with his brain cells than smoke them away. Then, to his brothers' pure joy, he said, "The man has never smoked a stem in his life."

"He's gonna love the Chronic!" shouted Franz excitedly.

"I think we should start him on Purple Haze!" countered Jack.

"We should let him try the Magic Kush!"

And then everyone erupted with his or her varying opinion on the matter simultaneously.

Fritz got everyone quiet again momentarily to finish up his story although Ernest had become so enflamed in his excitement that he had stripped naked and gone running into the wood singing "No Woman, No Cry" at the top of his lungs.

Fritz continued, "Then, with tears of joy and gratitude, he led me to the shore, where he had built a hut like Dankhurst on a small scale. I was impressed with his hut for it showed that our new friend has great skill and ingenuity. Around the walls he hung bows, arrows, lances, and bird-snares and on his worktable were boxes and cases, carved skillfully with a knife.

"These he told me were almost the only things washed ashore after the naval ship sank. Three years ago he was left here along with the ship's elderly captain. The old man passed only a few months ago. Still I was amazed by all they had accomplished together."

Elizabeth gasped and asked more about how they had come to this place.

"We'll have to ask the boy," replied Fritz. "I did not want to bombard him with questions. However, before darkness had fallen, he showed me all the ingenious inventions he had put in place—a kitchen stove, cooking utensils whittled out of wood, a smoke room from which meat hung in rows from the ceiling, bottles made out of hardened sand mixed with a bag of cement he'd found, shell plates and spoons, a fishing raft, and countless other things. We went to sleep that night, safe and well fed after he had prepared a delicious meal of crab and flamingo stew—the recipe for which, Mother, you must ask."

With that, my son wound up his tale, his voice trailing off until each of us had fallen deeply to sleep, happy and excited, each for his own reasons—Fritz for love, Jack for a taste of smoked meat, my wife for having found a new friend, Ernest for a new upcoming episode of *The L Word*, and I could not remember my reason, nor could I remember why we were on this island nor who these people were—but, there I was, happy and excited nonetheless.

CHAPTER 15

Turns Out, Edward Is Jenny

"We will find the perfect high. It will be a pure discovery. Jenny will find it for us."

The next morning we looked around for our breakfast, but my wife was nowhere to be found. Hungry, we looked blankly at each other, an underlying challenge to start chanting, "Breakfast, breakfast!" in every one of our eyes. Moments later, out of the cabin came my beautiful wife—and a seriously good-looking girl—each carrying a tray of turtle eggs and potato bread. The boys and I stared at them with a combination of lust and desire.

"Surprise!" said my wife. "Meet Jenny Montrose."

Jenny—not Edward—smiled shyly at us. Fritz looked at her with pure bafflement and no small amount of glee. I was a little bit relieved my kids weren't a bunch of fruits— even though I love gay people including Ellen DeGeneres and the guy from *Gomer Pile*—and I would have no issue if the kids liked it in the pooper—but what can I say? I was pretty happy to see that Mr. Montrose was a Miss and I *almost* kissed her inappropriately on the mouth to tell her so.

Instead I begged her to join our happy little life on the other side of the island.

But first Jack asked, "What happened to the guy?"

Then Fritz took over asking what we were all wondering. "Why were you pretending to be a man?"

"Pirates," she answered. "I couldn't let them think me a woman or Lord knows what they would have done. This naval uniform has been my only costume for the last three years." And thus, Jenny Montrose began her story—

Her mother had died in childbirth. Her father, a British officer, had left her with her grandmother while he went to serve in India. When she was just three years, her dad was lost to illness overseas. Soon after that, her grandmother followed to the other side.

After the death of his wife, her grandfather, a colonel in the King's Navy, centered all his love upon his only grandchild. They lived happily for many years.

Fifteen years later, her grandfather received orders to go overseas with his regiment. Jenny asked to accompany him on the ship. A week after they set sail, a storm arose and drove the vessel far off course. When the weather broke, their troubles were far from over. A pirate ship was fast approaching. With no time to spare, her grandfather fit her into an officer's uniform and cut off her long, beautiful brown hair. Ever since then she had kept it short. She blushed when she explained it made her feel safer, or, she explained, "Like a stronger version of myself."

The pirates killed all the servicemen but spared her life and her grandfather's, bringing them instead to the shore of this island and then leaving them for dead. For many weeks they lived awaiting the pirates' return. However, they never did.

From that time forth until our meeting, she never set eyes upon another human being. She kept a beacon continually blazing at the end of the reef in the hopes that someone would come to her aid.

"Who were the pirates?" my wife asked.

"I don't know, but they took our ship and abandoned us here."

My wife shuddered.

"For now," I announced happily, "we are all safe and even better, we are together. Please gather your belongings, Miss Montrose, and come with us to our leafy home."

With that, we all finished our breakfasts, watched as Fritz packed his canoe with everything he could take from Jenny's hut, boarded the boat, and made way for Dankhurst.

On the ride home while the others enjoyed the fine day and lofty views, Fritz came to my side and voiced his concerns.

"They'll be back," he warned.

"Who?" I asked.

The young man rolled his sober eyes. "The pirates, Father. Put that down," he swatted away the J I had put to my lips.

"Fritz!" I admonished and then calmly, knowing there was plenty more where that came from, I asked, "How could you possibly know they'll be back? It's been three years since they were last here."

"Well, the hydroponic greenhouse, for one, not to mention acres and acres of priceless cannabis. Father, you can be certain they will be back and when they get here they will not be happy about how much of their harvest we have already smoked—or I should say *you* have already smoked."

With that, Fritz crawled back to the "rudder" at the rear of the craft while I went back to steering the vessel with the faultless rudder of my mind. The rest of the ride was without incident. We showed the lovely Jenny Montrose our grass house with which she was delighted. Fritz promised he would build her a room at the top in the shape of turret like a castle.

"Fit for a princess!" he remarked gleefully, and behind his back his brothers made the motion of gagging themselves. Jenny, on the other hand, was quite gracious and seemed rather taken with my eager boy.

Fritz set to work immediately on the necessary foundation for a third-floor addition. He certainly had become motivated since he had arrived on the island. For a moment I wondered why as I sucked heartily on a cornucopia-size joint filled with the great bounty of our new and blessed home.

Jenny, who was quite adept at making useful the resources of the island (and we were down to our last box of Hot Pockets), took my wife under her wing, teaching her to prepare a delicious meal of Hot Pockets and wine from scratch, which blew Elizabeth's mind completely. We could tell the young woman wasn't as fond of the delicacies of American processed food as we Robinsons were, but we knew a way to help her understand why a neon-orange cheese puff trumped a lobster on the half-shell any day. We prepared a small bowl and then we gathered around her. Franz, being the most eager to please our new, comely friend, offered to light the bowl on her behalf.

Jenny took a deep breath and then held the bowl to her perfect pink lips. However, just as Jack went to light it, she waved his hand away. "Let me first cut away this disgusting green bit," she said with a little shudder. "See how it sticks to the sides of the pipe? No one should smoke anything so nasty."

"Leave the crystals, whatever you do!" I exclaimed. "Why, my dear, that is the very best part, and the delight of the true marijuana aficionado. Just ask Ernest." We looked to find my second son, but he was upside-down in a nearby tree with Nips hanging beside him. The two looked to be deeply engaged in conversation. Jenny now looked even more apprehensive than before. "If there really is too much," I went on, "just leave it for someone else to smoke."

Again Jenny assumed the position as Jack brought the lighter in for touchdown.

"What is this?" cried Fritz. "At least allow the girl to make her first time with a water-bong. We are fools to live so near the brook, and not keep one always full of clear water. How useful it would be!"

"That is a capital idea," I replied, "and we can use one from the ship or even make a new one if we can find clay so as to make a firm foundation in which to place the bowl."

"Oh, as to clay," said Jack, "I have a grand lump of clay there under that root."

"Well done, my lad! When did you find it?"

"Fritz found a bed of clay near the river a while ago," said his mother, "I had forgotten to tell you after what happened to me last week due to the incident with the Oreo filling."

"Well, Mother," added Fritz, "I can only tell you I never would have found the clay, if Ernest had not slipped and fallen in it."

"When you have stopped making fun of me," said Ernest, climbing down from his tree perch, "I should like to show you some plants I harvested yesterday. They are getting rather dry now. I have not ventured to smoke them, although our old pig devoured some of them at a great rate and then fell over with the most joyful expression on her face."

"How did you discover them?"

"I was wandering in the wood, and I came upon the sow grubbing under a small bush, eating something ravenously, and then dancing what seemed to be the Macarena. Knowing exactly what she had come across, I dove down and found a number of these plants, which I brought for you to see."

"Indeed, Ernest," I exclaimed, after taking the plants in my hand and considering them attentively, "I am inclined to believe that you have really made a brilliant discovery! If this proves to be, as I expect, the Sativa plant, we could lose every other smokable we possess and yet not want for anything. In the West Indies, they make bread from it, and so it also serves as a hearty culinary addition. Not to mention the fact that once smoked, you can play a very enjoyable bongo rhythm on your own belly!"

"How do we know if it's the Sativa?" asked Jack.

"Well, if we smoke it and our rumba becomes a cha-cha, we will know."

Jack then poised to smoke it, as if Ernest had said something sensible, until Fritz interjected. "But, you are all already high. Smoking now will only prove that when you smoke Ernest's plant with the Hydro from five minutes ago, you get a result *like* Sativa." We all had to sit for a moment as our minds were sufficiently blown by the brilliant Fritz.

"May I go on?" he asked. "Has that sunk in?"

We all nodded.

"In fact," he continued, "this has been the trouble with your pot experiments from the very beginning. You are all so blitzed twenty-four/seven, there's no way to gauge the effects of any of the marijuana you have been trying to organize."

"What do we do? Yeah, what's your idea, Fritz? How should we go about organizing ourselves? What do you suggest? How many licks to the center of a Tootsie Pop?"

"I say, we utilize our most pure resource," said Fritz.

"What's that? What are you talking about? I never was a Cornflake Girl!"

"Jenny," he said simply. "Let Jenny smoke only one joint of each strain per day and record her feelings."

We all muttered approvingly about Fritz's fine idea.

"We will find the perfect high. It will be a pure discovery. Jenny will find it for us."

Then one small voice under all the other voices said sincerely, "I have no idea what any of you are talking about, but can someone tell Ernest to please remove his fingers from under my armpit? He's tickling me."

We all laughed as Ernest pulled his hand away from the young girl.

Then we laid our plans for the upcoming day when our experiment would begin.

CHAPTER 16

A Pot Palace

Sure enough, from the ground the place had taken on the look of a castle with a turret at the top, fit for a princess.

The next morning Fritz set about creating an underground storehouse for our collected harvest. The young Jenny seemed eager to help him however she could. The rest of us, after smoking a fresh crop of Northern Lights, were less useful, but Jack found that his extreme focus made him a strong digger.

"I want you to know, Jenny," I overheard Fritz tell the girl, as we all stood by digging at our own pace, "I think you'll be okay on one joint a day; that's why I stepped in. I think you'll enjoy it, but you won't lose it, you know?"

Jenny nodded shyly, "Why don't you smoke one joint a day then, Fritz? If it's okay for me, or is it only fit for some of us?"

"Me?" said the boy grinning boyishly so that for a moment I thought him quite handsome and a rush of pride swelled in my breast. "I made a deal with Jah that if He rescued our family to someplace safe I'd make the greatest sacrifice of my life."

"But if Jah believes taking in cannabis as prayer, wouldn't you enact the opposite plan?"

I smiled to myself trying to look otherwise occupied as the young man thought carefully about his reply.

"This feels like the best way to display my gratitude," he said simply. And then reverted to his work installing supports and shelves in the cellar we were crafting—as if to end further discussion on the matter.

Using the sled, I moved a load of earth away from our site. As I walked, I thought about what Fritz had said. He was a principled young man—but then what were the rest of us? How had we said thank-you to our savior? I deposited my load and was slow in returning to Dankhurst.

My wife welcomed me joyfully, for she said I had so rarely come up with ways to help Fritz that she was truly proud. By moving away so much of the dirt from our cellar, our home was again clean and lovely. "Come home to rest," she said, "and think about what refreshment awaits you here inside the house. Come and see *my* cellar!" and she winked and led me to our marital bed inside our beautiful, fresh-smelling room.

When we were done, my wife presented me with a bottle of wine. Normally we drank it out of boxes, having finished off the Captain's stash weeks ago. "Ah! You wonder where this came from," she said. "Well, I found it on the sand today, while you all were busy creating the herb cellar. Fancying it was wine of some sort, I brought it to be a special treat for us. The boys will not get any." And she gave me a very sweet kiss.

Later we had a supper of delicious turtle meat prepared by our guest. We each enjoyed it so well that it gave us strength to bring out the mattress covers we had brought from the ship up into our sleeping-rooms. Then each of us, using mountains of buds from our island of plenty, stuffed the mattress covers until one was chubbier than the next. With Jenny's room unfinished, I slept in with my boys while she bunked with my wife. Despite being apart from my love, a refreshing slumber on my new mattress of glee closed the day.

Early the next morning, I got up without rousing any of the others, intending to go to the beach and enjoy a moment of quiet, baking up a little bowl of Maui Wowie. The dogs joined me and I tried to ignore their taunts, especially when Turk told me I looked like someone he'd like to eat. The flamingos flapped their wings; two little lambs gallivanted about. All around me life and energy erupted.

I noticed the cow was the only one not enjoying this clear fine morning, as she had not been milked in Lord knew how long. So I decided, to show my thankfulness, I would do it. Kneeling before her, I figured out how to hold the teats without laughing or causing her too much distress.

At the beach, I went to smoke my fine pipe, but something was troubling me. My son seemed so satisfied with his way of asking Jah for thanks. But what of me? What had I done? I had a beautiful, healthy wife. I had three wonderful strapping sons—and Ernest—and now we had a lovely daughter and an island covered end to end in all the marijuana of the world. I smoked up so that my bewilderment could be forgotten.

Approaching Dankhurst, I heard not a sound nor saw a soul. While not uncommon to sleep away most of the broad daylight hours, we had work to complete before we could begin our experiment. Then I noticed Fritz at the top of our house, making adjustments to Jenny's room.

"What have we here?" I asked, climbing up the new third-floor stairway my handy son had installed.

Fritz looked at me and then silently presented me a hammer. And so I helped as we laid planks and then coated them in a thick carpet of lovely dank weed. Fritz trimmed away a window out of one wall and hung hemp curtains he and his mother had fashioned for all the windows in the house. Jenny's curtains he had dyed a lovely shade of pink.

"Beet juice," he said by way of explanation for the color, as together we attached them around the glorious window of the small turret at the top of our castle.

Then we had completed the room, even adding a stuffed mattress to the corner with a small blue teddy bear the boy had secretly rescued from the wreck. Blushing ever so slightly, he left it set up against the pillow. Finally, on a table built from spare pot-bricks, the boy placed a hollowed drift-wood vase filled with fresh picked flowers.

The room was delightful. I placed my hand warmly on the boy's shoulder.

"She'll love it," I told him proudly.

"If she ever wakes up," he replied. "Where is everyone?"

"It must be the fault of those mattresses, they are delight-ful, but perhaps too lulling—everyone is still sound asleep."

Then winking at each other, my good son and I ran out-side and among the beasts and fowl, creating a deafening din among them.

Finally, with much stretching and many yawns, the other boys and my wife and Jenny at last came tumbling out of our delicious bud-abode, rubbing their eyes, half awake; Ernest was last, as usual.

"Come, family," I said. "Look and see what your brother the carpenter has fashioned out of our modest house to make it a castle."

Sure enough, from the ground the place had taken on the look of a castle with a turret at the top, fit for a princess. I glanced at Jenny and saw her flush with joy.

"Go look, my dear," I encouraged. And with that the girl flew back into the house. Moments later her bright pink cheeks appeared at the window.

"Oh, Fritz!" she called down to my blushing son. "It is wonderful!"

"I cannot take all the credit," he replied modestly. "My mother thought to dye the curtains and my father built the end table—sort of."

After the rest of the family paraded through, we reconvened outside in the fresh air.

"So now for morning bowls and breakfast," I announced, "and then off to work to finish our cellar and begin our experiment."

I encouraged everyone to take one of their mother's Adderall so that by dint of downright hard work, we accomplished the completion of a cellar to collect and maintain our harvest.

In celebration we decided to go for a boat ride before lunch. As we drew near Safety Bay, we were surprised to see a number of little figures standing in a row along the water's edge and gazing fixedly at us. They seemed to wear dark coats and white waistcoats, as if waiting to take our order. Every now and then one would extend his arms gently, as though longing to embrace us.

"Ah! Here at last come the inhabitants of this country to welcome us!" cried Ernest.

"Oh, Father!" exclaimed Jack, "I hope they are elfish! I once read a book about elves, so they must be real."

"You will have to give up the dream of elves and accept penguins, dear Jack," said his mother. "I have never seen so many. They are excellent swimmers, but helpless on land as they can neither fly nor run."

"Can we have one?" pleaded Jenny with wide eyes.

No sooner had she asked then out sprang Franz from the boat, and wading ashore, took the unsuspecting birds by surprise, and with a stick laid half a dozen, right and left, either stunned or half-dead at his feet. The rest escaped into the water, dove down deep, and disappeared.

As penguins are not good to eat on account of their strong oily taste, plus the fact that I was high on Early God Bud, which makes you extra-peaceful, I was sorry Franz had attacked. However, since he had smoked the Durban Poison, his strength was severely compromised and the fallen penguins arose from their swoon and began to solemnly waddle away.

However, Fritz was able to corral one into the boat where the bird sat gravely, looking about at his captors with a serious but resigned countenance.

Our approach set the dogs barking furiously, but discovering us, they rushed forward with such obvious demonstrations of delight that for a moment I wondered if Turk's bravado was secretly all a ruse.

I sent the boys to catch a goose to fasten to the penguin by the leg, thinking that it was worthwhile to try to tame him. Or at least it would be funny to watch.

My wife provided some homemade potatoes instead of her usual handiwork with the Hungry Jack mashed. Knowing that she had in her own mind pitted herself against the culinary artistry of young Jenny, I admired her work. She replied, "I wonder what you will say when I give you some Indian corn and melons and pumpkins and cucumbers!"

"I'll believe it when I see it," I replied, immediately taking note of the glare she sent my way. "I mean, I can't wait."

"I have planted seeds from the fields we have already discovered for a small garden," she admitted.

"And by 'I' she means Jenny," noted Fritz.

"Why, you are a model of prudence and industry!" I announced, ignoring the eldest boy, to which my wonderful wife blushed crimson and smiled.

"But," she continued, "I do not like the appearance of those mushrooms that are drying over by the creek. Is it possible someone plans to trip balls? I hope we make sure of an abundance of food for our mouths and pot for our lungs before we begin to think with our sixth senses!"

"I agree, Wife. I have not the remotest intention of using those shrooms as an everyday event! It will be a special treat to be used only when I say."

With that, all the boys but Fritz let out deep moans of despair. And then Ernest mumbled, "So, like starting tomorrow?" as he began chasing the trails he saw coming off his monkey.

"What possible connection can there be between tripping balls and mushrooms?" asked Jenny innocently.

We all laughed heartily. "Someday, child," said my wife warmly, taking the girl by the hand to have a walk in the setting sun. The rest of us went off separately to enjoy the evening. Finally night fell, and distributing ourselves throughout the castle of Dankhurst, we took to our beds and slept soundly.

CHAPTER 17

Baked . . . Bread

"If we ever make contact with the outside world . . . we are going to make a frickin' fortune in California."

When we awoke in the morning, we were ready to begin our orderly experiment. However, young Jenny was not.

"I'd rather make my attempt in the evening. Doesn't that sound much nicer?"

We were unable to argue with the logic that a toke fireside was a much more enjoyable way to smoke bamba for the first time than first thing in the morning—although Jack made a valiant attempt to argue it. Instead the girl suggested she teach us to bake bread.

"Just regular bread? Or like magic loaves?" wondered Franz.

"Oh, you must not expect *real* loaves," she said. "But on these flat iron plates I found in a crate that had washed up from our wreck, I am able to bake flat cakes or scones, which will be excellent."

Deciding it might make for a good day's distraction, we agreed. "First of all, I need you to make me a nice strong canvas bag," said Jenny.

We all just looked blankly from one to the other. Fritz, sighing loudly, set to work using the fine hemp fabric he had been spinning during all the months we had been on the island.

My wife, not putting much faith in her son's powers as a weaver, went out to help.

Then Jenny, spreading a large piece of sailcloth on the ground, summoned my boys and me around to set to work. She handed each of us what looked to be a cheese grater, two of which she had brought to our camp from hers and three more that she found in my wife's kitchen. Taking an ample supply of what the girl called "well-washed manioc root that grows abundantly on the island"—we heard it as "maniac root" and thought it an excellent name (when you're not a pretty young English woman, however, it is actually called cassava root)—and when all were seated on the cloth—"Ready, set, go!" Jenny cried, rubbing the root as hard as she could against the rough surface of her grater. At first my boys froze watching the young woman work with a crossed look caught somewhere between admiration and arousal.

A loud "Ahem!" from Fritz, who was watching from inside the house where he and his mother sat at the kitchen window enlisting the help of a sewing machine we had rescued from the wreck, brought us back to following our hot teacher's instructions amid bursts of laughter as everyone talked about the impolite gestures we made as each of us vehemently rubbed, rasped, grated, and ground down the roots. No one was tempted to stop and taste the flour, since it looked much like wet sawdust.

"Cassava bread is highly esteemed in many parts of the world, and I have even heard that some people prefer it to wheat bread. There are various species of manioc."

At the repeat of the name, another burst of giggles erupted from the boys. "One grows quickly," continued Jenny without missing a beat, "and its roots ripen in a very short time. Another kind grows slower. The roots of the third kind do not mature for two years. Before that they are poisonous if eaten raw—but I have heard that they are better and sweeter than the other strains."

"How do you use them if they are poison?" inquired Franz.

"You press them," answered Jenny knowledgeably, "in order to squeeze out the sap that contains the poison. Still, I never taste my cakes, until I watch their effect on a bird or a dog."

At that I saw Turk's head pick up off the ground where he and Juno had been lying. Certain he'd cast a glare upon our fine party, I changed the subject by asking Jenny where she learned her survival skills.

"My grandfather," she said somberly. "I never should have survived a minute on this island much less three years without him."

With that, we all decided we needed a bong break before continuing so that we wouldn't cry. When we returned, Fritz and my wife had taken up graters and our supply of roots had been sufficiently reduced to damp powder. The canvas bag was filled with it, and tying it tightly up, Jenny attempted to squeeze it. Jack took the bag from her to make his own attempt, but soon fell over panting and directed us that squeezing any liquid out of the root would require mechanical aid.

We watched as Fritz hauled my raft up from the beach. He placed the sack atop it and then above the sack he laid a wood flat. He then climbed up onto the middle and began jumping up and down. When he beckoned to her, Jenny jumped up with him. Holding hands, the two bounced and laughed. Then my wife and I joined in the fun. Unable to resist, my three younger boys followed as did the dogs, the monkey, and even the penguin-tied-to-the-goose—all climbed up on the contraption. There we each stood bouncing.

"How long until this bread spoils?" inquired my wife, who favored processed food to fresh. "Do we have to use everything in this giant bag at once? Will we have to spend the whole of tomorrow in baking cakes?"

"Not at all," replied Jenny. "Once dry, the flour will keep fresh for a long time."

"A Twinkie long time?" asked my wife skeptically, "or a frozen pizza long time?"

"Twinkie," said Jenny decisively and my wife's scowl melted into a full-face smile.

"Can we start baking now?" asked Jack who had clearly tired of jumping but didn't want to admit it to Jenny.

"We need to make sure there is absolutely no moisture remaining."

Climbing down off the flats and then coaxing the dogs, the monkey, and the penguin-tied-to-the-goose to do the same, we removed the top flat and discovered the moisture had in fact been sufficiently pressed out—or at least an English girl with a great ass said it was, which was good enough for us.

"But I will only make one cake today as an experiment," she said. "We must see how it agrees with Master Turk before we set up a regular bakery."

I tried to avert my eyes as the large dog grunted and then made for the woods with his faithful companion Juno, plus two flamingos, the sow, and the monkey.

Meanwhile, I took out a couple of handfuls of flour as instructed and placed it into a bowl we had rescued from our wreck. With a stick, Jenny loosened and stirred the remainder. My wife placed an iron plate over a good fire to heat up, while Jenny mixed the powder with water and a little salt, kneaded it well, and formed a thick cake. She laid it on the hot plate until one side turned an odd yellow-brown. She turned it and then quickly baked it in what we discovered was an actual stove in the kitchen we had never really been in. I had forgotten Fritz had convinced me to help him bring the stove from the wreck to shore by baiting me with a promise that I could use it to boil water for my very own hot tub.

The house began to smell so delicious, that we were all a bit envious of the two hens that were selected as tasters of the cake. We silently watched them gobbling up the bits of it, until I turned to Jenny, saying, "Suppose the cake is poisonous. What effect will it have on the creatures? Will they be stupefied, or will they be in pain?"

Jenny looked at me blankly for a moment, then noting that I was serious, shrugged and hummed *I don't know*, without words.

No sooner had the fowl been left picking up the last crumb they could find of the questionable food, we assembled to enjoy our afternoon meal of roasted potatoes, turtle meat Jenny had shown us how to prepare, and Ding Dongs. The potatoes were excellent, but the turtle had gummed up a bit and required a heavy hit off the Crystal.

Since Jenny insisted we wait until the next day to issue her decision for the rest of the flour, we decided to retire for a rest period before reconvening for our great experiment. While the rest of the family went off, Fritz led me down into the cellar to show me what he'd done.

The room was incredible. Every wall had been made secure from any kind of mudslide by a series of wooden planks taken deliberately off the wrecked ship. Fritz said I had told him to take them, but I had no memory of saying such a thing. Then he had built shelves attached with hardware he'd found at Miss Montrose's former dwelling. He used the jars and crates that the other boys and I had brought back after our last trip to the wreck and filled them with all the harvested strains we had thus far collected. Each had a label lovingly prepared by the labeler discovered by Ernest. Then, in alphabetical order, they were each displayed—AK-47, Blueberry Azura, Big Bud, Bob Marley, Chronic Supernova, Durban Poison, Early Misty, Easy Rider, First Mature, Hawaii Skunk, and on and on all the way to Zig-Zag Man. I was speechless. The boy had done well. With eyes full, I placed my hand on Fritz's shoulder as we scanned the incredible room.

"I have also added a trunk full of skins, bongs, bowls, lighters, and all the other paraphernalia." Sure enough, on the crate a clear label read *Paraphernalia*. I tried to muffle a sniffle as Fritz looked with a small smile at the floor.

"Why, Son?" I asked, knowing that this was no longer his playground.

My boy answered, with the utmost sincerity, "If we ever make contact with the outside world, Father, we are going to make a frickin' fortune in California."

After the sun had set, Fritz skinned up a tiny J out of the 4 Way since we roshamboed that numbers would go before *A* instead of after *Z*, and therefore, it became the first in the alphabetical order of our stash. He then handed it to his brother Jack to light. Jack carefully passed it to young Jenny who took a confident pull and was laid out in an extreme coughing fit in seconds. We all laughed as she regained her composure and finished the thing entirely.

When she was done, we looked upon her expectantly. Unsure what we were looking for, we simply watched.

"So?" Fritz asked.

"I . . ." Jenny didn't quite answer.

"Sometimes the first time you don't feel anything," announced my wife. We looked at her skeptically. "No, really!" she added. "I didn't."

"That's because oregano doesn't get you high," I chided.

The boys laughed, but Jenny laughed loudest of all. In fact, when everyone else had stopped laughing, Jenny continued loud and strong until all of us had no choice but to join her in laughter once again.

"Oregano!" she gasped. "That's hilarious!"

Jack, prompted by his oldest brother to get out his captain's log, wrote under 4 Way *Easily entertained*.

And thus, in good spirit, our experiment began.

The next morning Jenny slept in later than usual. When she awoke, she related to Jack that she felt great. No headache. Basically clear. She was clever enough to solve a series of math problems presented by Fritz. Jack made a final 4 Way entry that read *Clean hangover*. Once that was in order, everyone expressed great concern for the health of our hens, and we were thrilled when Jack, who ran to check on them, brought news of their perfect good health and spirits.

Our clearheaded Jenny began bread-baking in earnest. A large fire was kindled in the stove, the plates heated on the fire, and the meal made into cakes, each of us busily preparing our own and watching the baking most eagerly. Mistakes occurred, of course. Some of the bread was burned and some not done enough, but a pile of nice tempting cakes were soon ready, and with plenty of good milk, once Jenny showed us how to correctly milk the cow and preserve it, we breakfasted like royalty in the kitchen of our castle. Our spirits, if not our brains, were high with our success.

Soon after, Ernest, unusually sober, asked what was up with the bread.

"What do you mean?" asked Jenny.

"I mean, I'm not high. How is this maniac bread?"

"Mani-AHK!" said Jenny laughing, adding in an exaggerated American accent, "not mani-ACK!"

"What?" Jack asked, no one joining in on Jenny's glee except Fritz who had a little smile creeping at the corner of his lips. We all held out hope that maybe we just didn't understand her accent.

But realizing we had no idea what she was going on about, she clearly stated, "I'm afraid it's just flour, like wheat or potato. There is nothing else to it. It will sustain you nutrition-wise, but it will not get you high."

Dumbfounded, my family stared at this young lady, dismayed that we had been thus deceived.

"So we're not going to get high? Or we should keep waiting?" asked Ernest again hopefully.

"We're not getting high," answered Franz, getting up from the table and retreating outside to light up a spliff. Jack quickly followed, as did Elizabeth. Momentarily I, too, left the kitchen, motioning for Ernest to join me as the reality finally forced its way past all the damaged brain matter and into that place where he heard a voice chant, "Mayday. Sober. Mayday. Must. Smoke. Now."

Later, while feeding the poultry fragments of the remaining just-bread, I observed that the captive penguin was quite at ease among them and as tame as the geese and ducks. I loosened him from the goose and set him free. But I noticed he never again left the goose's side.

I don't know if it was the morning's disappointment or seeing all those birds running around like a bunch of turkeys, but it suddenly occurred to me what I wanted to do in order to say thank-you to Jah for the bounty of this great island and this great family of mine. We would dedicate an entire day to thanks and we would call it Thanksgiving.

CHAPTER 18

Seriously? Back to the Wreck?

We dragged the boat back to Hot Pocket Freedom Tent, where Fritz explained that I had super-secret ninja skills that no one expected but that might come in handy should the pirates ever come back for their extensive doobage stockpile.

Mere hours after birthing my idea for the new holiday of Thanksgiving, I completely forgot about it due to some particularly potent Aquaponic Jack had stumbled across. Instead, life on the island took on a normalcy that was quite pleasing for us all. We awoke each day, watched Fritz and Jenny do some work, received meals from wherever, and then each night administered Jenny her daily J and took down a report thereof.

One day Fritz decided that the rainy season was coming. I just figured he knew it because a light rain had begun. He reported that he would like to return for a final time to the wreck and all the valuables it still contained, feeling certain a destructive storm was imminent.

This time, everyone went.

The kids were delighted to go with the whole group and happily carried provision-bags filled with the-opposite-of-maniac-bread and potatoes.

Reaching Safety Bay without adventure, and, with the raft in tow, we steered straight for the wreck.

When we got onboard, everyone went his or her own way to collect whatever they could and load into the raft in time to return at nightfall. While Ernest and I were merrily caught up in a lightshow from the chandelier box, Fritz called out for assistance. We waited a while and when no one appeared to help him, we got up and found him wedged below deck in a small cramped space made further inaccessible by the rocks jutting inside the boat and the splashing of the waves.

"That," he said, pointing to pieces of what looked like a smashed-up Lincoln Logs set, "is a seaworthy craft—or else it could be made into one."

Of course, we simply stood there looking at the disembodied boat with wonder and confusion—our usual state of being.

"Room! Room to work in, boys! That's what we need in the first place!" he cried.

"Fetch axes, and let us break down the compartment and clear space all round."

"Who's Fletch?" asked Ernest. "I thought her name was Jenny."

"No, dude, go get an axe!"

And to work we all went, and though evening drew near, we made little headway on the mass of woodwork around us. We had to acknowledge that the amount of labor and perseverance necessary was not going to happen with the amount of Blue Dream we had brought on board.

Fritz, meanwhile, had managed to wedge himself into the impossible space and was proceeding to assemble the craft inside of its tomb until at last the fine vessel stood actually ready to be launched, still imprisoned within its massive wooden walls that defied our strength.

"What'd you go ahead and build it for? That was dumb. Now what? Is there an ice-cream sandwich anywhere?"

It seemed exactly as though the lovely craft had awakened from sleep and was longing to spring into the free blue sea, and spread her wings to the breeze. In fact, for a moment, I hallucinated that it had—because that is just how good the Skunk I was smoking was. When I regained my wits I continued with a thought I could not bear—that Fritz's success should be followed by an even greater failure and disappointment. Yet no possible means of setting the boat free could be conceived, even by Jenny who seemed like kind of a know-it-all. I was almost in despair, so I smoked another fatty when an idea occurred to me, which, if I could carry it out, would release the boat without further delay.

While everyone was busy—Fritz looking around wildly for something, Jenny and Elizabeth going through the trunks full of clothes and linens, Jack and Franz trying to figure out a way to play the Hendrix record they'd found, and Ernest trying on an enormous bra—I got a large cast-iron mortar, filled it with gunpowder, secured a block of oak to the top, through which I pierced a hole for the insertion of the match, and placed this item so that when it exploded, it would blow out the side of the vessel next to which Fritz's boat lay.

Then securing it with chains so that the recoil would do little damage, I told everyone it was time to go, calmly instructing them to get into the boat. There was some back talk from my eldest who seemed to think that sobriety meant he could condescend. I quickly squelched that idea by promising to reveal to the pretty Miss Montrose the thing I caught him doing behind the giant oak in our neighbor's yard when he was ten. He quickly made way for a seat among his brothers. Then lighting the wick, which would burn for some time before reaching the powder, I ran to join them with a pounding heart, and we made for the land.

We got to land before the thing blew and I decided I must have built it incorrectly, which would not have been a shocking revelation. But as we brought the raft close to shore and began to unload it, I listened with strained nerves for the expected sound. It came!—a flash! a mighty roar! and a grand burst of smoke!

My wife and children, terror-stricken, turned their eyes toward the sea, from where the startling noise had come.

"Pirates?" asked Jenny. "Are we under attack?"

"Perhaps," said my wife, looking at me, "perhaps you left a candle burning near something and an explosion has taken place."

"Not at all unlikely," I replied quietly. "I will go and see what happened. Does anyone want to come?"

Fritz needed no second invitation and sprang into the boat. We pulled out, heading for the wreck at a more rapid rate than we ever had before.

Nothing had changed on the side of the boat where we normally boarded, so we pulled around to the other side, where a marvelous sight awaited us. A huge hole had torn open the decks and bulwark. The water was covered with the exploded remains of the wreck completely in ruins; and the compartment where Fritz's boat rested was fully visible.

There sat the little beauty, uninjured by the explosion, and Fritz, who hadn't yet noticed his prize and was instead focused on the ruin and confusion around him, was amazed to hear me shout in enthusiastic delight, "Hurray! She is ours! The lovely boat you built is free! We can easily launch it now. Come, boy, let's set her free."

Fritz gazed at me for a moment and then guessing my secret, "You planned it *and pulled it off*, you clever father— even though you had smoked enough Blue Dream to marry the donkey! I am amazed that you knew how to build the explosive at all, much less successfully blow it up without losing a limb!" he cried. The young man eagerly followed me into the shattered opening where the launch could now be effected without much trouble. I placed rollers beneath the keel, so that we could move her forward toward the water.

Fritz organized a rope to create a pulley system by which we would get her lowered. Both of us agreed we needn't test our luck with my input at this point, so I retreated to smoke a bowl and stare at sparkly stuff. Finally the craft slipped gently and steadily into the water, where she floated as if it was her native element; while I, in my sudden rush of blitzed-out euphoria, went wild with excitement, cheered, and waved enthusiastically.

We dragged the boat back to Hot Pocket Freedom Tent, where Fritz explained that I had super-secret ninja skills that no one expected but that might come in handy should the pirates ever come back for their extensive doobage stockpile.

It turned out that Fritz had filled his lovely boat with all the weaponry he'd found on the ship—from little brass guns to real guns—Hawk semiautomatics, extensive stores of gunpowder, knives, seven broadswords that I was already imagining would be fun for Star Wars or Hamlet re-enact- ments, twelve axes, and an AccuSharp Knife Sharpener I was excited about trying out the broadswords—being familiar as I was with the infomercial. Jenny and the boys chattered incessantly about pirates, fleets of canoes, attack, defense, and final annihilation of the invaders.

I assured them that, brilliant as their victories would doubtless be, we should hope that their fighting powers and valor were never put to the test.

Fritz, however, who was the one stockpiling weaponry, was less sure. "Who do you think all this belongs to?" he asked. "Do you really think they've just forgotten about this place?"

"Who?" we all asked, my wife's eyes now wider than usual with alarm.

"The pirates! The guys who built all those greenhouses and Aquaponic gardens! The people who planted this place! Did *you* make it? Did *you*?"

We all continued to stare at Fritz, baffled. "Do you think a greenhouse grows from a seed that blew here from Asia?"

You could hear the crickets.

"I'm going for a boat ride."

Fritz jumped aboard his boat, guiding it swiftly through the water. I watched from shore, a ribbon of fear standing the hairs on my arms at attention. Ernest and Jack picked up two broadswords and immediately began a recreation of the battle scene in Episode Three where Anakin loses all his limbs to Obi-Wan.

Several more weeks passed and in our experiment, Jenny was still in the *A*s. By now, we were all used to vegging out without video games or TV. This was mostly accomplished by dressing up the animals, coating them in cool soup broth, and watching them go at each other. Jack was particularly good at "doing voices" for Turk and Juno as he mapped out a soap opera in which the two canine actors were the stars.

In the evening, we tried to encourage athletic exercises, such as running, leaping, wrestling, competitive eating, and climbing, so that we would all be strong and active, powerful, as well as agile and swift-footed. No one can be really courageous and self-reliant without an inward consciousness of his or her own physical power and capability.

"I want to see you all strong, both morally and physically," I said, then amended, "or at least just physically."

Jenny had by now completed a smoke house and a storage room for our instruments. She and Fritz had also built a wine cellar in which they had begun making wine and liquor from the generous fruits, nuts, and grains of the island.

One day we decided to hold a rodeo. This idea had come to young Franz in a dream he couldn't shake.

We began that afternoon. Taking a long cord, I attached a leaden bullet to each end, and instantly had to answer a storm of questions about what I was doing. (Whenever someone spotted me with a bullet, they generally were careful to inquire.)

"This is a miniature lasso," I explained. "You fasten stones to the ropes. Then one end is swung around and around and then cast with skill and precision toward the bull."

"That doesn't sound right," challenged Jack. "I thought you used a lasso to *catch* the bull by the horns."

"Well, yes, that, too. In *that* case, the lasso is thrown, while riding in hot pursuit, so as to make the stone twist many times around the neck, body, or legs of the bull, arresting him even at a full run."

"Are you sure, Father," asked Fritz, "or is that from a movie you saw?"

"Try it now," added Franz. "There is the donkey! Chase that ass. Catch some ass!"

Ignoring the uproarious laughter of the family, I was nervous and uncertain of my powers. Instead of practicing on a live subject, I decided to try aiming at the stump of a tree not too far away.

My success surpassed my own expectations. The stump was wrapped by the cord in such a way that it left no doubt whatsoever as to the possibility of catching an animal in the same fashion. Suddenly everyone was anxious to possess a lasso of his or her own, without a moment's delay.

Everyone made one, and lasso-practice became the order of the day.

Fritz, who was active and adroit and also had great muscular strength and the longest attention span, soon became skilled in the art.

That night, after everyone enjoyed a hookah while Jenny *really* enjoyed a joint full of Assassin of Youth—and has the rainbow-colored bruise on her hip to prove it—a change came over the weather. Early the next morning a gale of wind came up from the sea. From Jenny's upstairs turret window, I could see that the surface of the water was in violent agitation.

It was with no small satisfaction that I thought of our hard-won boat, safely moored in the harbor, and knew that there was nothing left on the wreck for us that we couldn't subsidize here on our island. And by "we" I meant Jenny or Fritz.

Jenny had spent time teaching Elizabeth how to preserve meat using lard and butter despite Elizabeth's profound devotion to disodium EDTA and calcium propionate ("It's what makes Stove Top Stuffing so delicious!" she's been known to insist).

It was during these rains that Fritz brought us out to the greenhouses where he tried to teach us how to help him keep our crops plentiful. "At the rate you guys smoke 'em, even an island as lush as this is at risk of extinction if we don't keep up with you."

Everyone was ready to do Fritz's will, having a vested interest by way of addiction—or in my case, just great a love and respect for all manner of cannabis since everyone *knows* there is nothing addictive about (excuse me while I smoke this) pot. Consequently the planting and tending of the fields and greenhouses was carried out with surprising vigor. We all agreed to make an early start the next day.

By sunrise we were all dead asleep. By noon Fritz finally had a coughing fit that woke everyone up and then we got ready to go for the next three and a half hours.

With the sled loaded with baskets of provisions, and pulled by the donkey, Turk, as usual, headed the procession, clad in his coat of armor, pretending as though we were his legion of slaves.

We crossed Skunk 1 and the magnificent country beyond extended in all its beauty and fertility before our eyes. We had never seen this enchanting part of the island before, although Fritz seemed quite confident among it.

While walking, Jenny amused us all by telling us the plotline of her favorite *Father Ted* episode, an Irish sitcom set on a small island in a church rectory. Everyone laughed heartily at the word *rectory*, although we didn't understand too much else about the story. Meanwhile, Ernest was standing apart under a splendid coconut palm, gazing up in admiration at the immense height of the trunk and its beautiful graceful crown of leaves. The cluster of nuts had him fascinated. I heard him exhale a long-drawn sigh, and the words: "I'm so high. I wish one of those nuts would fall down so I could eat it up." Scarcely had he uttered these words, when, as if by magic, down fell a huge nut straight onto his nose.

The boy was startled and sprang aside, yelling, "Oh, my nose!" then looking timidly upward. Another came crashing down and thwacked him in the head.

"Why, I'm gonna get you!" cried Ernest to the tree, holding up a fist in threat. "You are messing with the wrong Robinson!" and with that he began shadow-boxing a palm tree to our amusement as his nose reddened and his eyes began to darken underneath.

"I suspect the fairy in the tree is trying to pelt you away," laughed Jack, lighting a joint to share with his unfortunate brother. Then a young orangutan revealed himself to be playing with us—after which he immediately began playing with himself.

As we went on, our progress became increasingly difficult. We were stopped by having to clear hanging boughs and the creeping plants that interlaced them. Ernest continued to lag behind, which was annoying as usual and kept requiring that Fritz go back and get him moving again.

After struggling onward for a short time, we emerged from the thickets onto open ground and saw two of the greenhouses in the distance. As we drew near, their man-made appearance much surprised and amused us for we had become unused to things like glass and cast metal. But we were speedily at the door, and Fritz organized us and taught us to plant, harvest, and prune. He explained he had already killed quite a few plants teaching himself what worked best. Everyone was given a job most suited to his or her skill set. Jack was meant to cut, Elizabeth to bundle the harvest, Jenny to sow new seeds, Franz to prune bushes and clean the glass, and Ernest to "taste" as he himself put it. I was dispatched to name the varietals as the one who, since the age of eleven, could tell which cannabis plant stood before him by image, smell, or taste. Fritz oversaw.

After we completed our work in one greenhouse, we moved together into the second.

When it was time to dine, Fritz and Jack built a fire. Their mother thought this a perfect time for them to cook for themselves. Because they could make use of four cans of Campbell's Cream of Mushroom soup, two bags of Tostitos, and a jar of salsa, they agreed.

The cooking operations soon came to a standstill after the fire was lighted, for there was no water with which to loosen the condensed soup and Franz's idea to use the bong water was squelched by his straightedge brother. When Jenny suggested using coconut milk in place of water, all the boys cried out, "Grody to the max in Cocoa Puffs!" while fake-gagging themselves for extra emphasis. So we agreed to go in search of a spring.

Very soon after our exploration began, Ernest, who was at the front for a change, turned with a face of terror, shouting, "A dancing bear! I mean, a wild boar, Father! Come quick!"

And, sure enough, I heard a loud snorting and puffing as some large animal ran hastily through the wood. "After him, after him!" cried Fritz, hurrying forward. "Call the dogs! Stand ready to fire!" Unsure what to do, given that among us we possessed a wooden spoon, two joints, and a pack of Fred Myer matches, we decided to hide in the bushes until the thing passed.

Fritz managed to tackle what proved to be a large respectable-looking pig, by holding on by the great ears, while the animal, upon seeing us, appeared happy rather than desperate to get away.

In a moment, the truth became apparent. The captive grunter was no fierce native of the forest, but our own runaway sow that none of us had noticed had run away! Our excitement caused Ernest to squeal in a high-pitched tenor that sounded not unlike a twelve-year-old girl at a Justin Bieber concert. We all felt a little angry with the creature that had abandoned us to begin with—then we got super-blitzed on the rest of the dank so that the absurdity of the whole thing made us laugh. We even gave the old sow a little to celebrate her return and to see if it would make her stumble hilariously into trees as it had the monkey.

Our laughter resounded through the wood. A good deal of joking on the subject ensued, and since in all this time not a drop of water had been discovered, and our thirst and hunger were increasing, even Fritz agreed we had done enough work for the day and could head home.

The boys, as promised, made a hearty meal out of the soup and nacho chips. Then, after a somber joint of Astro Turf that made Jenny first go into fiercely boring detail about a childhood dream to play the cello in a rock band and something about the fluoride in the water being the reason for all the fine teeth in America, we had all earned our pleasant night's sleep.

CHAPTER 19

A New Thanksgiving

*. . . I had never been this fucked up
in my life.*

The first thing to be done on the following day was to return to the greenhouses to finish the harvest.

I alone accompanied Fritz. Passing through a veritable forest of New Purple Power, Fritz discussed what could be done to tame the wild growth. We passed our pig feasting on acorns, as oblivious of us as ever.

Back in the greenhouse some plants attracted my notice, as their crystals were so plump and large they looked almost like small white berries and the buds were very sticky when plucked. I recognized it immediately as a plant called Goof Butt by rappers and queens alike, and with much pleasure, I explained to Fritz that, by straining these crystals, we might easily succeed in making our heads detach from our bodies and float unheeded into the sky, which even if he couldn't appreciate, his mother would.

Fritz meanwhile was focused on another nonagent of THC that produced a greenish wax he claimed might be "useful." We fought momentarily about the definition of "useful" and then were at least able to agree that the wax smelled quite good regardless. We lost no time in harvesting enough of each plant to fill one large canvas bag a piece. We then continued our work.

After attending to the hydroponic species, Fritz took me out to a nearby field. While I was lost with my nose in a fragrant patch of Wonder Woman, Fritz yet again had been lost to a grove of perfectly useless, if tall, trees with very strong, broad, thick leaves. As he examined them, he found they bore a round figlike fruit, full of sour little seeds.

Fritz saw some gummy resin exuding from cracks in the bark, and when he told me, I got excited again because of the words *gummy, resin,* and *exuding from cracks*—all together and separately. He attempted to soften what he'd collected in his hands but found it could stretch and then spring back to its original size.

"Father, look! It's very elastic! I think this is latex."

"What!" I cried. "Let me see it! What a valuable discovery that would be!"

"Why would it be so very valuable, Father?" inquired Fritz, the sarcasm dripping in his words.

"Er . . . sex toys, corsets . . ." I almost said, or *did* say, based on the look of horror that spread across my son's face, so I modified my reply. "India-rubber is a milky resinous juice that flows from certain trees in considerable quantities when the stem is tapped correctly. The natives, who first obtained it, used it to form bottles by smearing earthen flasks with repeated coatings of the fresh gum and when hardened and sufficiently thick, they broke the mold, shook out the fragments, and hung the bottles in smoke, until they became firmer, and of a dark color."

Fritz rendered speechless by my thorough answer added toughly, "Yeah, and also we can use it to waterproof the greenhouses—not to mention, do some work on Dankhurst."

Soon after making our discovery, Fritz had tapped the tree and was taking up a collection of the sap in coconut shells. While he did so, he allowed me to get super-blitzed and try to move the leaves in the trees with my powers of telekinesis, which totally worked of course.

At one point, having mad munchies, I saw some fat worms and maggots and, remembering that in the West Indies they are eaten as a delicacy, I put some in my pockets for later.

When we got back, an excellent supper was ready of crab and flamingo stew made by our Jenny, who later partook of her first of the B's, B-52, to rather uneventful results, including a period during which we all fell asleep for about ten minutes according to Fritz. So with thankful hearts, we all enjoyed the dinner together except Elizabeth who would only eat a Jimmy Dean's breakfast sandwich—even though we were down to our last box. Then, climbing the grand stairway of our castle, we ended this fatiguing day.

The next morning we each awoke, one after the other. Fritz, however, had a crazy look on his face—a wide smile and shining eyes.

"What's the matter with you?" we asked, "Did you smoke something? Why are you smiling like that? Is anyone else wearing a thong?"

Fritz, still smiling, said, "Why, it's our anniversary!"

"Whose?"

"Ours! Ours and Jenny's!"

The young man was beaming so beatifically at her that Jenny could do little more than blush.

"That's it!" I cried out like a person who has finally remembered something he had been meaning to remember for a while. "We must celebrate—not just meeting Jenny, but the great fortune that led to our meeting! I have wanted to follow Fritz's example of great respect for Jah Almighty for quite some time. Tonight we will celebrate the first Thanksgiving."

Everyone let out an unusually motivated cheer, so I went on, "I expect us all to contribute to the event."

Fritz decided that he would focus on making candles so that the party would be alight with beautiful little fires. Jenny promised to bake something delicious using her nonmaniac-flour that she swore would be ultramaniacal! Meanwhile, my wife promised to attempt a meal that did not involve sorbic acid.

I had a splendid idea that cost me several hours lost in the woods until I found it—the Magic Kush. None of us had ever smoked it. And even though Jenny was only on *G* in terms of our experiment, I knew there was no better night than during our great celebration. As I went about cutting and harvesting the plants, it dawned on me that there wouldn't be enough time to dry out the buds sufficiently. Then I remembered that Ernest had taken some with him the first time we had come upon the patch.

Making haste back to Dankhurst, I found Ernest busy scratching his back on the bark of a palm tree while singing "Silent Night" in Spanish.

"Where's the Magic Kush?" I asked him, prepared to spend the rest of the day helping him find it, even if it meant taking our fine house apart.

"I gave it to you," he answered. "You put it in your bag."

He was right. And after a moment of rifling through, I pulled from the back pocket a small wooden box, inside of which was stuffed the dry buds of this great plant.

Our house was alive with delicious smells, from Jenny's baking to Fritz's lovely green sweet-scented wax to my wife's culinary inventiveness. I sat for a moment just enjoying the fragrance of gratitude.

After the candles had hung in a cool shady place to harden, Fritz arranged them throughout the kitchen and across several strings he had hung to light up the outside. For the first time, Dankhurst was brilliantly illuminated.

The women came out wearing new clothing—but being men, none of us noticed until Jenny said, "Isn't Elizabeth's new dress lovely?" I realized then that had been why I couldn't stop staring at her breasts. Then my wife replied in kind, "Isn't Jenny's hair growing out beautifully and don't you just love her fabulous new hemp jumper?"

The supper was presented outside the castle, at a spot where we might have a good view of the sunset. Darkness came on, but our candles kept the air alive and bright.

"How beautiful!" exclaimed Jack. "I hope they burn until morning."

"Not very likely," Fritz replied. "I didn't have any animal fat to harden the wax. I'd say we have three hours tops."

"I don't think we'll need light," I added. "I have arranged for a dessert that ought to produce all the light we need." With that I revealed the leaves of Magic Kush and saw even Fritz look upon it rather wistfully.

We lit a large fire and soon supper was prepared. Jenny's bread, it turned out, this time contained beautifully rendered pot-butter and, she promised, would likely be a fantastic hors d'oeuvres. We tucked in—as did, I noticed, Fritz. I clapped him on the shoulder and let him know telepathically that on, of all days, Thanksgiving, Jah would want him to express his gratitude with a nice dose of THC.

My wife's dinner was a delectable ham cooked to perfection with a host of potatoes and a rich stuffing she'd produced without the help of Stove Top, but instead—corn and several shrooms from the patch by the river. When asked where she'd gotten the pork, my good wife replied sheepishly, "I was sick of that damn sow."

Just as the bread and stuffing began to take effect, I took out the Magic Kush and skinned up seven small joints. We each, including Fritz, smoked in silence as the lights he had strung up in the trees began to flutter and die. The children started laughing and couldn't stop—all except Ernest who looked around, saying, "What? What's going on?"

I stood up and offered my hand to my wife who took it and together we floated among the Big Bud plants that surrounded our home to a song only the two of us could hear—"Blame It on the Rain" by Milli Vanilli. Everyone dispersed in various directions; some to stare at things, and some to play with each other's hair. Ernest, however, had started writing out math problems in the dirt and solving them quickly.

Soon we reconvened and together shared bong hits of the Magic Kush. This time, the monkey appeared followed by the penguin and his best friend the goose who all gazed up at us with longing eyes.

"We can blow it in their faces," suggested Jenny.

And so we did. Soon the boys had gone missing. We discovered them high up in the trees. My wife and Jenny went to join them.

"I am not such a young athlete," I cried. However, not wanting to be left alone, I began to climb, surprised by how quickly I reached the summit.

Once we had all taken our position on the wide, safe branches, young Jenny announced she had another surprise for us.

"Bravo!" I cried. "I love surprises!"

"Here," she said, "is a wine that the greatest connoisseur would prize. Taste it."

The shell was filled with clear rosy liquor, bright and sparkling.

My wife tasted it first. "Excellent, excellent," she exclaimed. "To your very good health, my dear girl!'"

We drank the rosy wine in turn, and Jenny received hearty thanks from all. We sat lazily for a while in the tree until all of the sudden a small voice said, "Um, guys? I don't feel anything."

We looked around for the source of the voice and discovered it was our Ernest, who, it was true never looked more sober in his life. All of a sudden, Fritz burst out in hysterical laughter. We looked on, waiting for him to collect himself and express his thoughts.

"Ernest . . ." he managed between gasps, ". . . finally blew his mind back to sobriety!"

Understanding that Fritz meant that Ernest had smoked himself sober, left us no choice but to join in with great belly laughter of own—all but Ernest who only punctuated our hysterics by asking, "What?" and "Why is that funny?"

By the time our laughter abated, it was getting late. When we got everyone down from the tree, a feat helped by our dear Ernest who was even able to carry his mother to the ground, his dexterity was so good. Once at the bottom, our donkey suddenly shocked us all with a loud bray, and without the least cause, he galloped off into the thicket of weed plants.

I was annoyed by this, and a little alarmed, because not only had we lost ourselves one great ass, which I said out loud and for which I got a hearty chuckle, but I had never been this fucked up in my life.

After everyone sat in the grass enjoying his or her own version of Pink Floyd's "The Wall" to an imaginary screening of *The Wizard of Oz*—except Ernest who had gone to look for our donkey—we all passed out.

A bright morning awoke us early to a series of moans and no fewer than four renditions of "I'll take my hair of the dog straight up!" Ernest however looked great, pink cheeked and wide-awake. "I'm going to go check the fields," he announced as he bounded off.

The rest of us tried to keep down breakfast, and, then, without further discussion, each one of us went up to our rooms and back to bed.

CHAPTER 20

A Stoner's Fantasy: The Perch in the Sky

. . . a porch swing and hemp linens dyed bold colors for decoration, along with strings of lanterns and intricate beadwork taken on by the seven of us during bouts of motivated self-expression were presented in glorious display—IKEA-catalogue style.

When we arose the next day, Ernest was awake and bright-eyed, waiting for us impatiently in the kitchen.

"I've been chasing ass for the last twenty-four hours," he said soberly, "to no avail."

With a few unstoppable giggles coming from the group behind me, I asked, "You mean, you can't find the donkey?"

"I can't find the donkey, and now I am going to smoke a fatty and forget about it."

With that, my second-born climbed the stairs and left the rest of us to organize breakfast. My wife used the bacon Jenny had smoked from the remains of our old sow. Meanwhile, Fritz was explaining to the rest of us that the donkey was a great asset, which of course was funny because he said "asset," so we all agreed to spend the day looking for him. We ate together, then leaving my wife and Franz behind, set off.

For an hour or more we trudged onward, directed by the print of the ass's hoofs. Sometimes we lost his track for a while, only to discover it again upon reaching softer soil. Finally this guide failed us altogether, for the donkey seemed to have joined with a herd of some larger animals, with whose hoof prints his had mingled.

We almost turned back in despair, but the children urged us onward. Jack pointed out that "if we climb a hill, we will be unable to miss so large a herd as this must be at almost any distance."

I consented, and we again pushed forward, through bushes, sometimes cutting our way with an axe, and sometimes plunging knee-deep through a swamp. Eventually we reached the border of a wide plain, and on it, in the distance we could see a herd of animals, grazing on the rich grass. It seemed likely to be the very herd to which our good donkey had joined himself, and so we resolved to make a detour through a field of Misty Bud to get as near as possible to the animals without disturbing them.

The plants were huge, many of them over ten feet in height; and, as we made our way through them, I remembered an account of this strain, that it is one of the originals and according to legend, brought one a terrifically cerebral high.

I explained this to Jack, and we discussed the possibility of cutting several down and carrying them home.

By then we had reached the edge of the field where we found ourselves face to face with the herd—a herd of buffalo. They looked up, and stared at us inquisitively, but without moving. "Move back," I said with my mind, understanding the danger inherent in a herd of this size.

As it was getting late, and I was suddenly excited to harvest a bit of the Misty for later, I encouraged the rest to give up the search for the ass and to return to our camp.

We again made our way through the field, but before we left, I cut down a few of the bigger stems.

As we walked, there was a set of footsteps coming up behind us. When we turned to look, there stood a buffalo calf that had been timidly following us through the field. Fritz pulled back to make certain none of the larger creatures had come with it, and when he found none, he verily covered the infant's large head with a rope and walked it along with us.

The new animal delighted everyone immensely and, in their opinion, amply compensated for the loss of our poor donkey.

We arrived back at Dankhurst in time for supper, and as we sat at that meal, for which we were heartily thankful, my wife and son packed bowls so that we might refresh ourselves for the first time in too many hours.

As the sun set below the horizon, we were enjoying the antics of a menagerie of pets. Franz had found an eaglet he wished to tame, but no one knew how. Fritz wanted the eaglet, too, so a deal was struck. "I tame the young bird to keep as my own, and if I succeed, I will give you Nips the monkey in exchange." Franz thought for a moment and not having any idea how to begin to tame the young eagle, agreed to the terms. With that, Fritz took a pipe and filled it with Hawaiian Haze, a good choice—hypnotizing and mellow—and sucked the smoke into his mouth but no further, then he blew it out all round the bird's head, so that it had to inhale until it became stupefied, and its savage nature subdued.

He sat beneath the bird, which struggled furiously, and puffed cloud after cloud around it, and as each cloud circled around the eagle's head, it became quieter and quieter, until it sat quite still, gazing stupidly at the young smoker.

"Whoa, dude!" we cried, as Fritz hooded the bird.

"Excellent, Fritz," admitted Franz. "So I guess Nips is mine."

Before bed, Jenny had her evening joint—this time of B-52 From Fantasia—after which she performed a short piece from *The Lord of the Dance* and turned in.

The next morning the children and I did our work in the field using our buffalo as the beast of burden—dragging our materials to and fro.

I think my good wife was fairly shocked at the way we fell upon the pizza and palm-cabbage, made by Jenny, she set before us for lunch. We explained we were thrilled since we had smoked some of the Hydro on our way home, which is known to cause the most severe cases of munchies. As we sat reclining after our labor and digesting our meal, we discussed the various projects we might attempt.

"I wish," said my wife, "that you would invent some other plan for climbing to the top of the tree from within the castle. I think that the castle itself is perfect, but I would like to be able to look out from the high tree without having to pull myself up on branches. Could we fashion a flight of steps to the top and perhaps make up a patio in the canopy above?"

I carefully thought about how my wife would have looked delivering that speech naked while the children discussed how they might go about completing the project.

"It would be lame," said Fritz, "to make stairs outside the tree, if we could build them *within* the trunk. Ever since Jah has accepted my thanks and asked me back to smoking," as he had been doing again since our Thanksgiving celebration, "I have been thinking how totally awesome it would be to hollow out the trunk, and climb up and out to a balcony that doubles as a lookout perch since from that high bough you can see the bay."

"Oh, yes," said little Franz. "I want to hollow out the old tree and build a staircase!"

"Well, now, the trunk may already be sufficiently hollow to allow us to begin, for like the willow, it might draw all its nourishment through the bark, and I think if we smoke some of the Aurora Indica, which the lovely Jenny taught us last month is good for discipline and focus. Excellent whittling, by the way," Fritz said, pausing to pick up a fork from the seven-piece utensil set the young lady had accomplished. "We might begin our work at once."

After the whopper of a J, Jack sprang to his feet to go and study the mammoth structure that served as backbone to our castle. The rest of us followed his example, and the other children were all soon climbing about like squirrels peeping into the hole at the base of the tree and tapping the wood to discover by sound how far up the cavity extended.

They forgot, in their eagerness, that something was living in this trunk. They were soon reminded of it, however, for the bees, disturbed by the noise, with an angry buzz burst out and in an instant attacked the nuisance. They swarmed around the children, stinging them on the hands, faces, and necks, pursuing them as they ran to me, my wife, and Jenny—who had not been high and therefore had thought the better of joining them—for assistance.

We got rid of the angry insects by blowing bong hits of Venus at them, after which we were able to attend to the boys. Jack had fared the worst and his face swelled to an extraordinary degree. It was only by the constant inhalation of Space Queen, an anti-inflammatory strain, which luckily grew in abundance near Hot Pocket Freedom Tent, that he was able to function over the next few days. Afterward, the boys were less eager to commence an organized attack upon the bees, so we all decided to wait until after we ate some snacks.

In the meantime, arrangements were made to relocate the beehive. Jenny suggested using a large gourd for the new beehive. Nothing more could be done, since the irritated bees were still angrily buzzing around the tree. We waited until dark, and then when all the bees had again returned to their trunk—with my assistance watching from below and offering instruction with my mind—the children carefully stopped up every hole in the tree with wet clay, so that the bees would not leave the tree before we could begin the operation.

After Jenny smoked a joint of Bahia Black and discussed at length how her body had turned into Jell-O, we couldn't resist joining her—and then, there in the grass we fell into a dead sleep.

Since we were out in the bright sunlight we were up early and working. Fritz first took a hollow stick of bamboo and inserted one end into the tree. Then, filling up his lungs with schwag, he steadily blew the smoke into the trunk.

The humming and buzzing within was tremendous. Even though I was using telepathy to explain, the bees did not understand what was going to happen. Soon the buzzing quieted and subsided into a murmur. By the time Fritz had finished his fourth bowl, all was still; the bees were stupefied. Unfortunately, so was Fritz.

So, Jenny, in his stead, cut a small door into the wood by the side of the hole. She opened it carefully and removed the insects, as they clung in clusters to the sides of the tree, and placed them in the hive she had prepared for their reception.

With the bees now magically removed from the trunk, and relocated to another tree, Jenny scraped the honey from the honeycomb and poured it off into jars and pots. Then after a hard day's work and Jenny sampling the Baked Alaska to generally euphoric results, we turned in.

The internal architecture of the tree had now to be attended to, and early the following morning we prepared for the task of cutting out our stairwell. Using the door Jenny had already made, Jack and Fritz set about clearing out the rotten wood from the center of the trunk until, as we stood below, we could look up the trunk, which was like a great smooth funnel to the sky above.

It was now ready for the staircase. First Fritz erected a stout sapling to form the axis around which we would build the spiral stairs. Jenny took over when the boys fell apart on the harvest of Dawgy Style and cut out notches for the steps and corresponding notches in the tree itself to support the outer ends. She then formed the steps using planks we had somehow collected from the wreck—mostly by accident because someone thought a knot here or there resembled a celebrity and had brought it back to show his mother. Using a hammer, the industrious girl was able to pound them into place without nails.

Upward and upward she built, cutting windows in the trunk, as she deemed practical, to admit light and air, until we were at the topmost branch, on which Jenny felt a lovely balcony might be constructed.

This task occupied us for the whole next year. But at the end, another Thanksgiving had arrived, and in all that time with the abundance of weed on the island, Jenny had only made it to the Ds. But Dankhurst now featured an impressive porch with a porch swing and hemp linens dyed bold colors for decoration, along with strings of lanterns and intricate beadwork taken on by the seven of us during bouts of motivated self-expression presented in glorious display—IKEA-catalogue style.

We did not entirely neglect the details of our colonial establishment that year. Somehow, the animals were mostly attended, as were the fields and greenhouses. Thanks to Jenny, we were beginning to know better which strains were best to take and when—and passed them around accordingly.

Our endeavors to keep ourselves busy worked well. Our mornings were occupied in tending the plants; in the afternoons we all amused ourselves sometimes autonomously and sometimes collectively.

In the evening, when our home was illuminated with wax candles, we kept journals of all the events that had occurred since our arrival in this foreign land, or we painted, spun hemp, or sang Smooth Jazz hits of the '80s and '90s.

Week after week rolled by. Week after week saw us joyful and content. Incessant rain in the rainy season battered down above us, and yet the scene as viewed from above was a merry one.

CHAPTER 21

The Great Race

The first to reach Hot Pocket Tent
was to bring back proof of his success—
a back issue of High Times *I had*
accidentally left near the pond.

Thanksgiving night we celebrated on our new balcony. Although the rain fell steadily, the sealant Fritz had made from our endless resin supply kept us dry and content. By morning, the winds were lulled and the sun shot brilliant rays through the clouds as the rain ceased to fall.

Our plantations were by some miracle thriving vigorously. The seeds we had sown were shooting through the moist earth. All nature was refreshed.

We decided to take a walk together and enjoy our expansive lands. We rambled along a new path and came upon a large cave that led into the belly of a mountain. Fritz and I enlarged the opening, and using the candles Ernest had taken to bringing everywhere he went due to a newly acquired fear of the dark, Fritz and Jenny led the way, banging the ground as they went with a long pole to feel for any great hole or chasm.

Silently we marched—my wife, the boys, and Jenny— awed by the beauty and general sparkle of the scene. We were in a grotto of diamonds—a vast cave of glittering crystal. The candles reflected on the walls a golden light, bright as the stars of Heaven, while great crystal pillars rose from the floor like mighty trees, mingling their branches high above us and drooping in hundreds of stalactites, which sparkled and glittered with all the colors of the rainbow.

At one point, we all fell to our knees, overcome by the beauty. The floor of this magnificent palace was formed of hard, dry sand. I tasted it for no other reason than that I was hungry. That's when I discovered that this was a cavern of rock-salt.

Disappointed it wasn't diamonds, we filled a few bags with it anyway to make beef jerky and left for home.

Lunch followed soon after, during which we discussed what we missed most back in civilization. Jenny missed facials. My wife missed Pringles, and all four boys and I in unison named our favorite sport. I missed football. Fritz missed baseball. Franz missed soccer. Jack missed basketball. And Ernest missed synchronized swimming. All our talk soon led me to a great idea, perfect for spring—tomorrow we would begin what I called, "A Grand Display of Athletic Sports," quickly given its acronym, AGDAS, that soon became simply "AGAS" for which my wife and I would serve as both spectators and judges.

"What a great idea! Can we run races? And get prizes! Will there be prizes? I want one of those stretchy rubber faces out of a box of Cracker Jacks!"

"Yes, we will offer prizes for the competition in every event," I replied, deferring the questioning eyebrow from my wife until later. "What events shall we have?"

"Shooting," suggested Fritz a little quickly.

"Running, riding, climbing, and swimming," added Jack.

"Leaping," said Ernest.

The children all began to bustle about, rolling up joints containing the strains of their choosing that they thought best suited to physical exertion. Jenny, who still had a lot of strains to go in completing our grand experiment, settled for stockpiling the ever-hydrating milk of the coconut.

That night, the events of the coming day were all anyone spoke of. Jenny's joint of Diablito led Franz to roll up a few joints to add to the others he'd rolled out of Afgooey X Haze.

Everyone found it difficult to sleep that night and come morning, it was like holding back horses in the gate.

"Let us start with shooting first and start the rest when the heat of the day declines. Here is a mark we got ready for you," I said, proudly producing a board roughly shaped like a police officer and about the size of one. This target was enjoyed, but Jack was not satisfied until he had added a hat, a muscle shirt, and a long leather strap for a holster that gave me pause remembering how well the boy had responded to *Edward* Montrose.

The target was then placed at a good distance for firing. Each of the four competitors was to fire twice.

Fritz hit the cop's head each time; Jack hit the body once; and Jenny shot the hat clean off his head, which raised a shout of cheer. Ernest was disqualified for sticking his tongue into the barrel of the gun and giving his mother a near–heart attack.

The second event with pistols involved the competitors shooting at a mango thrown as high as possible up in the air and trying to hit it before it touched the ground.

In this we found to our surprise that young Jenny succeeded quite as well as her suitor, Fritz.

As for Jack, his mango escaped wholly uninjured. After this followed a game of pool on a table Fritz had built out of pot-bricks and hemp a few months before to impress Jenny. In this practice I saw with pleasure that my sons were really skillful. Even little Franz played well. Jenny, on the other hand, got bored and forfeited the game.

Next we started the running match. Fritz, Ernest, Jenny, Jack, and Franz were to run to Hot Pocket Freedom Tent by the most direct path. The first to reach it was to bring back proof of his success—a back issue of *High Times* I had accidentally left near the pond.

At the signal, the racers ran off in fine style. Fritz and Jack put forth all their powers and took the lead at once, running ahead of Ernest and Jenny, who had both started at good steady paces that they would be better able to maintain than such a furious rate as the others.

In the meantime, my wife and I got away with a quickie. We then went off to dig up prizes. Luckily, the genius I had married had a whole feast of wonderful gifts for the children. But before she could reveal them all, a tremendous noise of galloping caused us to look with surprise toward the path where Jack made his appearance, thundering along on the buffalo, now fully grown and powerful.

"Hello!" I cried. "What kind of foot-race is this, Master Jack?"

He shouted merrily as he dashed up to us; then flinging himself off, and saluting us in a playful way, he said, "I very quickly realized that I didn't have a chance, so I caught the buffalo, and made him gallop home with me in time to see the others come puffing in."

Soon the others arrived, Franz holding up the magazine, having won the race.

Next came our climbing race. In this exercise, Jack performed wonders. He ascended with remarkable agility to the highest part of the palm. From there he behaved like a true idiot, mimicking a squirrel or a monkey until we were all laughing uproariously.

Fritz, Ernest, and Franz were bored early on and went to feed their munchies with several boxes of breakfast bars we'd recently come across hidden inside a guitar case in the musical instrument storage room. Questioning their "staying power" over two-plus years on a damp island, they had been put into a clearly labeled "munchies food" stash instead of into our general stores on the off chance that someone sober might unwittingly eat them. Jenny climbed well but could not come near the grace and skill of our Jack.

Riding was our last game where marvelous feats were performed. Fritz rode on the back of the donkey that had at some point wandered back to camp. Jack rode his trusty buffalo. Franz was clever enough to hop onto an awkward-looking saddle wrapped around our fun-loving kangaroo, who looked, in the moment, to be in sore need of either fun *or* loving. Ernest spent most of the race trying to make a tree branch run. And young Jenny, with few options left, mounted the cow.

Then each taking up a whip, and holding tight to their beasts, at the word *go*, each rider prodded his or her animal to walk, trot, and gallop. At some point during the awkward and messy race, Ernest appeared laughing uproariously on the back of the horrified Turk.

He miraculously pulled ahead with only a few short lengths to go, and with that, our dim Ernest won the race. I still don't know how he managed it, but as they passed the finish line I am certain the dog flipped me the bird with an enormous middle claw.

We ended the day with swimming-matches to cool off our contenders. Pretty soon, however, the seriousness of the games disappeared and everyone simply played among the rocks and waves. At one point Elizabeth tapped my shoulder and pointed my gaze to where Fritz had taken Jenny's hand and pulled her in close. Then as waves swelled around them, he kissed her gently as she wrapped her arms around his neck. My wife squeezed my arm and kissed me happily.

By this time, as it was getting late, we returned to our dwelling, my wife having gone ahead of us in order to make arrangements for dinner.

We ate a lovely meal of roasted hen and potatoes with a guava and cheese salad and a few of Jenny's leftover maniac-bread cakes from Thanksgiving. Afterward it was time for Jenny's pot experiment. We skipped the Diambista strain, knowing that it was only one step up from smoking oregano and moved right on to Dimba. After Jenny described it as pleasant but a little bit warming, it was time for the ceremony of prize-giving.

My wife began handing out the prizes one by one. Fritz, to his immense delight, received as the prize for shooting a pin with a peace sign on it, which his mother nobly added to his lapel, along with a bullet that she had made into a necklace, strung up on a piece of dark brown leather cured from the pig's hide that she let Jenny tie on.

Ernest, as the winner of the riding match, was given a saddle she had also fashioned out of the leather hide of the sow with help from Fritz and Jenny.

For Jenny, she had repaired her grandfather's antique pocket watch. Overcome, Jenny's eyes welled up and she hugged Elizabeth gratefully.

For climbing, Jack received a little wooden stash box his mother had carved.

Franz received a bell that had come off the ship to do with as he pleased, but not while people were chilling.

When the ceremony was supposed to be over, I stood up and solemnly presented to my wife a small box into which I had placed several precious stones I had found and saved and forgotten about from the captain's quarters. Within were settled diamonds, emeralds, and rubies out of which I hoped we might be able to manufacture some lovely baubles for her to wear or simply to zone out staring at as the sun danced across their facets.

The ceremony was not yet over. All of our children led my wife and me up the grand staircase within the tree to the porch overlook at the top. Within, we discovered an array of candles lit up in torches. The chandelier from the wreck had been strung up and hung, making glorious prisms across the branches of the tree from the candlelight. But most wondrous was that somehow the children had made up a bed in the room surrounded by all of our things in place of the porch swing.

"A master bedroom," said Fritz.

My wife, with great tears of happiness coming down her face, embraced each of our children who then snuck out and left their two old parents to enjoy themselves in solitude at the top of the world.

The next morning we discovered that our children had rearranged themselves within the castle. Fritz and Jenny were now sharing the old master bedroom—an ulterior motive my wife and I had not foreseen but about which we were both thrilled. Meanwhile Franz had taken over Jenny's old room in the turret. Ernest had been sleeping in a nearby tree for almost a year now, so Jack kept the boys' room for himself.

I recollected that it was now the time when the Widow-rella plants would be ripe. We set about harvesting immediately, as it was Jack's favorite strain. On our way we came across a huge flock of wild pigeons. Fritz used his rifle and newly awarded shooting skills to procure dinner.

After we ate, Jenny announced she had a prize for us. My wife asked if we might all enjoy it from the master bedroom at the top of the castle.

Agreeing, we all climbed up the spiral stairwell to the perch where my wife opened up several bottles of wine.

"Based on my studies," began Jenny, getting everyone's attention, "I have come up with a special treat for each of you. For all that you have done for me, saved me, loved me"—at that her eyes met those of my eldest son—"I can never thank you."

She passed to each of us a perfectly rolled joint.

"In each," she went on, "is what I believe to be the perfect mixture of cannabis strain that falls between *A* and *D* for each of you. For our sweet mother, there is Afgooey to lessen her arthritis mixed with a small amount of Bangkok Diesel for pizzazz. For our noble Father, Brainstorm Haze, to keep his long term memory, and what remains of the short term, in good working order, with a dash of the Black, for soul. For good Jack I have made a sunny mix of Bee Neck and Cryptonie. Franz gets a straight shot of Dynamite since he is . . . well . . . dynamite. My great friend Ernest gets Crazy Weed for obvious reasons. My perfectly beautiful Fritz gets Dream and a little bit of Ace sprinkled over top. And for me, a little Belyando Spruce for my cramps." At the last one, all the boys groaned, and Jenny and Elizabeth rolled their eyes and grinned in female solidarity.

We each bid Jenny a hearty thank-you and lit our joints, except Jenny who was still needed for experimentation and promised to smoke hers only as needed, which prompted a second series of groans from the boys.

That was when we heard in the distance a terrific din, like something exploding beneath the surface of the ocean. Perched on our lookout we could see the black water, but could not make out anything on its surface.

"Pirates," whispered Fritz, and all of us froze and looked at him. A wide surprising grin spread across his face. "We are going to be rich!" the young man called as he flew out of the perch and down the steps, leaving the rest of us to wonder how we were to be rich if pirates were shooting and we were going to be dead.

In the frenzy that followed only one thing struck me. It was the look on the face of our dear Jenny as Fritz cried out again from the ground below in great cheer, "We are going to be so so rich!" And Jenny whispered wistfully toward the sea, "I thought we already were...."

CHAPTER 22

The Pirates Return

"Are these pirates looking to be featured on QVC?"

The next morning arrived after little sleep. Fritz had disappeared, leaving the rest of us anxiously awaiting morning glow to see into the distance. We all must have dozed off as those first few rays came up from behind the great blue.

"I see something in the distance, Father!" cried Jack, awakening us all with a jolt. "Do you think Fritz is right? That it's pirates? I think I can make out the top of a mast, then it sinks, and the water coils along. It does seem as if it is coming toward the island."

My wife took alarm at this and put her hand on my arm. Knowing that Fritz was off doing Jah-knew-what, I decided to take charge. I told everyone to close up the castle and keep watch with firearms at the upper windows.

Fritz returned by and by and hollered, "By what means will sitting with your guns at windows defeat seventy men with semiautomatics?"

With that Fritz climbed up through the tree stairwell and made his way to the lookout. Then using the captain's telescope, and with a broad smile, he shouted, "It is, as we feared, an enormous pirate ship!" The young man spoke with less fear than palpable joy. "It advances directly this way, and we shall be placed in the greatest possible danger, for it will cross the bay for certain."

"Should we attack it?" asked Franz.

"Only with the greatest caution," returned Fritz. "They will be far too formidable for us to rashly attempt their destruction. Thank Jah we have the advantage. They do not know we are here. We can keep in safe retreat, while we watch for an opportunity to destroy this frightful enemy. Mother, I charge you with remaining here at the perch. We must monitor the monsters' advances. Franz, you must always stay within earshot of Mother, and in the event that a warning must be issued, you are to run on foot and alert us."

Fritz led the rest of us unwillingly away from our safe haven.

"Why are we attacking, boy?" I asked as I followed Fritz into the jungle.

"What do you suggest, old man? That we let them kill us?"

"How do you know they will kill us?" asked Jenny, her face set in serious disapproval of the whole matter. "They did not kill me or my grandfather when they brought us to this place."

"But they left you here to *die*, did they not? And look at all that we've taken from them!" Fritz cried, splaying wide his arms at the great island we had smoked pretty much to pieces.

"But we have also given," I added quietly.

"Yes," agreed Jenny. "We have tilled and harvested, cut back overgrowth, and sown many seeds. Perhaps they will value our work."

"We have to kill them," decided Fritz. "Kill them, take their ship, and go to California."

Jenny's eyes briefly met mine and I saw that they were bright with tears.

"Where are we going? How much farther? Anyone bring a bat? Or a one-hitter? I'm hungry! I have to whiz." And thus went the conversation.

As we went, I recollected how easily it would be for the pirates to pass through our walls if Fritz was right and they meant us harm. I thought of my beautiful wife and hoped Franz would be able to take care of her. But if the boat advanced, there was no word about it from Dankhurst.

Fritz led us in a direction I did not remember, which didn't say anything as I was not always capable of forming new memories. Finally we reached a cavern. Suddenly Jack exclaimed: "I think this is a second cave of salt! See how the walls shine! And how the light is reflected from the roof!"

"These aren't salt crystals," said Fritz, "the water flowing over them leaves no track and tastes quite sweet. Taste it for yourself."

Ernest immediately fell to all fours and with his tongue to the floor, lapped at the glistening rock as though he had just walked off the face of the sun.

"Oh, how splendid!" said Jenny, changing our focus. "Then we have discovered a great treasure! We can barter diamonds with the pirates for our lives!"

"Why wouldn't they just kill us and take it if we showed it to them? How do we know they don't already know it is here? And anyway, why would they leave us in peace in exchange for what isn't even true diamonds but cubic zirconia? Are these pirates looking to be featured on QVC? I think not," said Fritz decidedly.

By then we had entered a back room where a large opening allowed in great streams of sunlight. Throughout the room was a staggering store of weapons—gunpowder, bows and arrows, gasoline, and an untold number of knives, rocks, and guns. Everyone gasped.

"We can defeat them," said Fritz. "I've been waiting for their return. . . ."

With that, he began handing each of us boxes full of his stockpile. Then he led us back out of the cave. Jenny, however, did not emerge with the rest of us. As Fritz marched on unknowingly, I went back. I found the girl using a hammer and a chisel. She was on her knees trying to remove a clear and beautiful crystal off the floor of the cave.

"I will break off a piece for a specimen," she said. "See, here is a fine one, only rather dull, and not transparent. What a pity! I will knock off another."

Approaching her and kneeling down, I said gently, "You must be more careful, or the second will look as dull as the first. You destroyed its true form, which is that of a pyramid, with six sides or facets."

The two of us remained for some time in this interesting grotto, pretending some great horror was not about to befall us. But soon our light burned low and Jenny, having secured a large lump that exhibited several crystals to perfection, knew it was time to go. Fritz, by then, was returning for his second trip with Jack and Ernest in tow. He picked up a small pistol and discharged a few shots for the sake of hearing the grand echoes. Jenny turned angrily to return to Dankhurst with her load. She didn't appreciate the playful air with which Fritz was taking things.

Fritz followed her and took her by the arm, saying, "I am doing this to protect us."

"Then let's not fight them!" retorted Jenny.

"But what if they give us no choice?"

"Then, okay, *then* we can fight. But give them a chance. See what they want. Let them come to the island and then let's follow them and see what they do. . . ."

I could see that Fritz did not like this option, but because I knew he loved the girl, he agreed. "But we must be prepared," said Fritz. "Promise you will help to prepare Dankhurst for battle."

Jenny, administering a giant kiss on Fritz's mouth, agreed. And we thus set off.

On reaching the outside, we saw poor Franz breathing heavily as if he had run a long way, but as soon as we appeared, he ran toward us.

"My child, what is the matter?" I asked anxiously.

"The pirate ship has reached the bay! Mother sent me to get you."

We all hurried back to Dankhurst where Fritz issued orders. Ernest and Franz were sent to fill coconuts with gasoline-soaked rags to make small bombs. Fritz and I were dispatched to pile our fire logs at the top of the mountain overlooking Rubber Band, the islet where we anticipated the pirates' approach. Fritz had devised the hold ingeniously with a hemp net thrown overtop sixty or more full-size logs, which would prove a peril to any man below.

Nearby, Jenny contrived an aqueduct, for a similar purpose, that water might be damned and released in a rush onto our visitors.

Pipes of hollow bamboo answered a different purpose. Jack was dispatched to dip darts in gasoline that would be lighted and loaded, and then blown at the pirates as they closed in. Fritz had done well. Our supplies were good, and the comfort of having so much with which to defend ourselves, even led my wife to declare that she was well pleased with our engineering.

Casks and barrels of all sorts and sizes were also pressed into service, filled with rocks and similarly tied to a high point from which they might be released with destructive force until every pirate might be knocked to pieces.

That night the weather became very unsettled and stormy. Heavy clouds gathered on the horizon, and passing storms of wind, with thunder, lightning, and torrents of rain, swept over the face of nature from time to time.

The sea was in frequent commotion; heavy groundswells drove masses of water hissing and foaming against the cliffs. The pirates would have to wait for this weather to break before any attempt could be made at a good, safe anchor.

We agreed that two would hold watch while the rest slept that first night. Jenny did not move on to the *E*s as scheduled, as she did not feel much like experimenting. Since no one else felt like toking up either, and we were so unused to sleeping without an herbal aid, not much sleeping was to be had at Dankhurst that night.

I met up with Fritz and Jenny in the lookout, preparing to garrison our fortress in warlike array. We reinforced the weapons at the openings throughout the castle, after strongly barricading the windows and entrances of the bottom floors.

Fritz suggested we make every attempt to lure the pirates to Dankhurst and use the element of surprise to our advantage.

Jenny did not like this plan and rather hoped we might just stay hidden until the pirates got what they wanted and then set off again. A compromise was reached whereby Fritz and Jenny would follow the pirates at a safe distance until their intention became clear. If they were only here to pick up a few things and go, Fritz agreed (even though he had great plans for that seaworthy vessel they brought with them) to let them be.

Not wanting the children to be overly exhausted come morning, my wife and I insisted they smoke a bowl out of the Roor bong we had bought at auction from Michael Phelps, and catch some rest. We promised to reawaken them should the weather break and the ship make a move.

Elizabeth and I continued to watch from the perch, while Fritz and Jenny went to sleep. Ourselves unseen, we sat in darkness, masked by the camouflage our castle provided. We then spent the rest of the night awaiting with beating hearts the further advance of the foe, which, for the time being, remained invisible to us.

CHAPTER 23

The Great Distraction

NO ASSES ALLOWED.

For three whole days we were kept in suspense and fear, not daring to move more than a few hundred steps from our front door, although during all that time the enemy never made landfall or in any way showed signs of their presence. Only from the height of our perch could we even see the rising and falling of the top of the mast in the distant sea.

In fact, we might have forgotten about them entirely and gone back to our way of life—smoking by day, sleeping by night, and eating in between. However, the air was so alarmingly charged that even the Magic Kush could no longer keep our anxieties at bay.

The boys alleviated some of this energy by swimming anxiously about in the pond and showed their uneasiness by dunking each other more forcefully than usual, even growing violent during their games of Marco Polo so that their mother and I had to separate them so that each could get his breath.

My uncertainty increased, as time passed on. Fritz espoused that the arrival of this ship meant we had to claim ownership of the island outright. If we waited for these interlopers to lay claim first—seeing as it was probably their grass to begin with—we might lose everything. However, I could not imagine my small family, for whom I had so much love, venturing to attack so potentially formidable a foe. Yet it was dreadful to live in a state of blockade, cut off from all our important duties—like trying to mix a little bit of Buddha with Trainwreck to see if we felt more peaceful or more–train wrecked. Jenny and Elizabeth had perfected their Hot Pockets–from–scratch recipe, since our store had run out months before—so there was pepperoni to cure and cheese to curd. Not to mention, staying shut up in the unnatural light of the pot castle, we were enduring constant anxiety and perturbation—which is not the good kind of "-urbation."

Out of this painful state we were momentarily distracted by none other than our good old simple-hearted donkey—not Ernest, but the actual donkey—who was hardly to be praised since his action came by sheer stupidity.

With no activity to report from the still-distant ship, we had all agreed that we needed to severely smoke the shit out of some major doobage. So, the next morning we skinned up the rest of the available stash and packed a few bowls. While the rest of us were so engaged, my wife opened the door to take hers outside. No one noticed when the old ass, fresh and frolicsome after a long rest, suddenly bolted free, careening at full gallop straight for the marsh.

In vain we called him back, worried he would make for the beach and reveal us to the enemy before they had even disembarked from their ship. Fritz would have rushed after him, had not I held him back. In another moment the ass stood close to the thicket of Blueberry Bud we had planted last spring, and that's when things got totally weird.

"What is that?" exclaimed Jenny, with a cold shudder of horror. Had the pirates tricked us and arrived at the island without our noticing? Were we doomed? Upon further study, however, it was plain our pirate-vigil had not been in vain.

However, what we beheld still caught all of us by surprise. An enormous snake, perhaps fifteen or more feet in length with a body in the middle that it would have taken no fewer than six grown-men's hands to encircle, emerged out of the bush and with fiery eyes, its dark deadly jaws opened widely, the forked tongue darting greedily forth—and the poor ass's fate was sealed.

Becoming aware of danger, the animal stopped short, spread out all four legs, and set up the most piteous and discordant bray that ever echoed from rocks.

Swift and straight as a fencer's thrust, the destroyer was upon him. It wound round him, entangled, enfolded, compressed him, all the while cunningly avoiding the convulsive kicks of the agonized animal.

A cry of horror arose from the spectators of this miserable tragedy.

"Dude!" cried Franz.

"No way!" added Jack.

"What?" asked Ernest.

"Our old friend is lost to us for ever!" cried Elizabeth.

"Will the beast swallow it all at once, Father?" cried Franz. "I just blew a huge bowl of Chronic. It will be too shocking! I don't know if I could take it."

"Snakes only have fangs, so they can't chew their food and must swallow it whole," said Fritz. "But it isn't any more shocking than watching something get torn and shredded like lions and tigers do to their prey."

But, truth be told, it was *incredibly shocking* to watch the monster deal with its victim—pulling it closer and more tightly curling and crushing until the bones gave way and the animal was virtually kneaded into a shapeless mass. By now we were all furiously smoking away at our stash, staring at the show in great satisfaction-mixed-with-horror.

"Look! He is gorging his prey, and slowly but surely it is moving down into that unhinged jaw!"

My wife, with little Franz and sober Jenny, found the scene all too horrible and ran back into the castle, trembling and distressed. To the rest of us there was an incredible fascination that accompanied the dreadful sight, and we could not move from the spot. I hoped that the boa, before swallowing his prey, would cover it with saliva, because it would get all shiny and cool looking, although it struck me that such an endeavor would take a long time considering that the very slender forked tongue would make about the worst possible implement for such a purpose.

Unfortunately, the act of lubricating the mass must have taken place during the process of swallowing for nothing was applied beforehand. This wonderful performance lasted from morning until noon. When the awkward morsel was entirely swallowed, the serpent lay stiff, distorted, and apparently insensible along the edge of the marsh.

"Did anybody ever think of eating serpents?" inquired Fritz.

"That is nasty!" said Jack. "Did you see what that thing just did to that donkey?"

I was feeling a little hungry myself, and since our stockpiles were low having been held up at Dankhurst for so many days, I found myself agreeing with Fritz. "First of all, the boa is not poisonous, but besides that, the flesh even of poisonous snakes can be eaten without danger—like the rattlesnake, from which you can make a strong and nourishing soup, tasting like very good chicken broth. Of course, the cook must throw away the head containing the deadly fangs."

My diatribe had lost the attention of two out of the three boys. But Fritz, taking up a loaded gun, approached the animal amid the most intense food-coma any of us had every witnessed and firing but once into the head, killed it. We then set about filleting long pieces of it, avoiding the midportion inside which our poor donkey's ass was decomposing.

Fritz took one half of the meat and added it to our smoke house where we would later cure it and turn it into beef jerky—or snake jerky. The rest he brought to the kitchen and asked his girlfriend to make into a luscious lunch.

We rested in the shade of some rocks for a considerable time. The open air was welcome to us, so much so that the ship in the bay was all but forgotten.

In fact, we spoke gaily of the snake-charmers of India who fearlessly handle the most deadly of the serpent tribe, the Cobra di Capello—or hooded cobra—and induce them to move in time to musical sounds from a small pipe. Jack ran and got a pipe out of our musical equipment room—as opposed to a pipe out of our Paraphernalia box—that we kept for spontaneous drum circles and played it well enough that soon Ernest was dancing in a serpentine fashion and making everyone laugh, whether or not he was trying to do so.

"To get Ernest to dance in this state, no instrument is required," we agreed.

After a while, a quiet, tearful retching was heard. Our Jenny was crying.

"We have to memorialize the donkey," she said when we all stared at her in alarm.

"Yes!" we agreed. "Who can give us an epitaph for our unfortunate friend? We must afford him more honor than he is presently enjoying."

Jack took the matter quite seriously, and planting his elbows on his knees, he bent his thoughtful brow in his hands and remained in poetic meditation for about two minutes.

"I have it!" he cried.

"Don't be shy, old boy, spit it out!" and thus encouraged, with the blush of a modest author, he began:

Beneath this stone a poor bony ass is laid,
A faithful ass it was, and loved by all.
It was useful for sitting and dragging around,
Until a snake wrapped 'round it and led to its fall.
It was hard to miss, an ass like that—
It was a great ass to watch and a great ass to catch.
But we, though yet mourn our honest ass,
And are ever grateful for all the grass!

"Hurray for the epitaph! Well done, Jack!" we applauded, and taking out a large red pencil, I inscribed the words on a great flat stone so we wouldn't forget them—as we were even then forgetting a boatful of nearby pirates.

We then ate our delicious lunch of snake soup, after which we cut free the mangled remains of the ass and buried it in soft marshy ground close by and filled up the hole with fragments of rock.

We arranged the head of the serpent with the jaws wide open, to make it look as alarming as possible.

Over the rock we inscribed these words: NO ASSES ALLOWED.

And the double meaning of this sentence pleased us all immensely.

CHAPTER 24

The Ostrich Weapon

*Jack and Ernest . . . agreed in thinking the
moving objects were men on horseback.
I was thrilled to be able to pronounce
them to be very large ostriches.*

The greatest danger was yet unfolding. However, that anxiety had slipped my mind and the minds of my family.

It was morning again and Fritz had thought to revisit our lookout. At his bequest, we all made our way up the staircase in the tree, myself breathing quite heavily as I was experiencing early-onset emphysema. Reaching the perch we found Fritz, ashen faced and looking out at the sea where no mast could be seen.

"Where have they gone?" my wife asked.

"Did no one see them leave?"

"What if they have not left but are somewhere moored to the island?"

"My underwear is riding up. Is anyone else's?"

"Let's go!" I said, suggesting we make two excursions—the first to make a thorough examination of the shoreline, and the next to the greenhouses, where the archenemy could have entered our territory.

Fritz and I left the others and made our way to the marsh. Nothing was discovered here and no rushes, grass, or bog-plants were beaten down.

We followed the streamlet from the rocks to the seashore. However, before we made it there, we were momentarily distracted by our munchies.

"I found a young serpent," said Fritz. "It is over there covered with rushes; it is nearly four feet long, and as thick as my arm."

"A serpent!" I cried, my hunger getting away from me. Instead I uncovered a fine large eel, which would provide an excellent supper for us if we weren't about to be under attack by pirates.

We made our way down to the shore easily by keeping close to the cliffs, where the ground was firmer. It was most important to ascertain whether the ship had docked or sailed on. Being unable to get a clear look from the beach, however, we directed our course upward.

We arrived at the crest of the rock ridge just before nightfall. All was peaceful and in good order. No trace of the boat could be seen in any direction. There were no signs of visits from pirates. When we passed by the greenhouse, both the little farm and the inhabitants we had planted within looked most flourishing.

We returned home and prepared our unagi for dinner. The next day passed in surveying the immediate neighborhood, while at the same time, collecting a quantity of Banana Kush, which we wanted for its pleasant aroma and calming nature. Fritz again served as my companion, carrying a small gun in case we were met by our uninvited guests.

We went slowly along the left bank of the lake, winding our way among weedy thickets.

Just then a harsh booming sound struck our ears. I paused in wonder as to where the noise had come from, while Fritz exclaimed, "Oh, Father! I think they are upon us!"

"And they are firing at us?" I asked, beginning to tremble after listening attentively for a minute or two. "I am inclined to think they are just fooling around. They cannot know we are here."

"I want to shoot them all," the boy mumbled quietly, cocking his pistol. He was very anxious and seemed to be waiting with readiness to fire.

"There is nothing we can do from here," I whispered to the tense young man. "We must approach them from the sea. Tomorrow we will set sail from the beach and wind our way around the island to this place where we will see what our friends are doing."

"Our friends," laughed Fritz sarcastically. However, we resolved to make it the object of our excursion the next day, excited to pursue this adventure. We readied the boat as it required some repairs.

We set out, carefully, quietly, this time allowing Turk and Jack to accompany us. The island being steep and rocky, it was necessary to be careful, but we found a landing-place on the far side. The boys hurried to the beach where they could easily climb the cliff face and get a view, while I clambered to the highest point I could climb on land—to avoid scrambling up cliff faces.

On rejoining my sons, I found them already on top of the mountain, angling for a view of the ship, which from here was clearly moored below us.

"Isn't she a great brute!" cried Fritz, referring to the pirate ship, the skull and crossbones waving in the wind. "She is ever so much larger than she seemed from a distance."

"Well, let us amuse ourselves watching them for the present," I said. But Fritz was quick to counter—"I see that at least one life boat has been dispatched, which can only mean that some of them have already made landfall. I agree that a lookout must remain here; however, I will go into the forest and see what I can of those who have disembarked.

"Jack, you stay here. This is now your perch. Father will send Franz as the runner between you and Dankhurst. And I will return home by morning."

Leaving my brave boys, I prepared to return to the boat. Jack seemed excited about remaining alone with Turk on the hill to await Franz, explaining that it made him feel just like Chuck Nolan in *Castaway*.

To this, however, I let him know that our fate, as a family stranded on a desert island, was adventure enough and beseeched him to remain invisible from his perch.

I found it hard work to row back, mostly having left the heavy lifting to the kids. I had to exert my wonderful inventive powers to contrive some kind of rowing machine.

"You lazy fellow!" I mumbled to myself.

However, I soon managed to get myself back around the inlet to our familiar beach where I tied off and made my way home.

Presently, hearing shots in the direction of Dankhurst where I had left my wife and family, I ran quickly. I was relieved to find that they had only killed a small wild pig, which would prove nice for pepperoni Hot Pockets and pork rinds.

After dinner I sent Franz back to the lookout where his brother watched our pirate friends. I knew that I would feel better if the boy passed the night with company. And should the need arise, one of them could be dispatched to report any dangerous behavior without leaving their perch entirely abandoned.

Jenny, clearly nervous, went about Dankhurst occupying herself with the smoke house, where she both smoked and smoked pork.

She continually expressed how pleased she was with the space, which was roomy enough to hang all our salami and bacon. On a wide hearth in the middle, she kindled a large fire, kept constantly smoldering by heaping it with damp schwag. The hut being closed in filled with smoke, which penetrated the meat thoroughly. We thus occupied ourselves for the day.

Finally, as I was getting ready to return to the perch where I'd left two of my most precious possessions, Fritz returned, followed in short order by a breathless Franz.

"They're going!" cried Franz.

"They're staying!" countered Fritz.

We looked from one boy to the other, hopeful that the younger had the true story.

"We saw them return to the ship and pull up the anchor!" Franz argued.

"They left behind a group of men who have discovered us. They seek us even as we speak. More than likely the ship is going to explore the island until we are discovered."

"What do we do?" Franz asked.

"Go get Jack," said Fritz. "We must prepare for battle."

The barricade was first inspected. We resolved to make our defenses doubly strong, being convinced that they were fortified and foolproof so they might resist the invaders we dreaded.

Where they were expected to emerge from the rocky pass, we intended to station Jack and Ernest with the stockpile of coconut bombs we had fashioned. The swelling hills were fortified with bales of heavy tree trunks—where Elizabeth would be stationed with an axe to cut them free when the order was given. Jenny was sent to unleash the dam and flood the valley where the intruders would end up before reaching Dankhurst.

Meanwhile, Fritz procured a massive amount of rope to complicate any escape by wrapping it about the trees all around the outside perimeter of the valley.

Their march proceeded slowly. We had no way of knowing when the pirates would arrive. Meanwhile, Fritz and Franz went to meet the ship at the water and accomplish whatever damage they could using their guns and the camouflage of the island for protection.

When I saw a coconut fly, lit up by the wick and then popping in a slight—if somewhat scary—explosion, I called out, "Patience, my good fellows! You are too easily affrighted. Look beyond to those grand mountains sheltering us. It will be some time before our foes make their way to our pot enclave."

After gazing for some time on the distant scene, I passed out some of our provisions so that we were busily engaged for some time, when Nips began to sniff and smell about in a very strange way.

"Is it possible that I see a party of horsemen riding at full gallop toward us?" asked my wife, who I was pretty sure had not hit the good stuff since the night before. "We have to be on our guard, whatever they are," I replied.

"I can't see distinctly enough to be sure," she said, "and with my imagination fragile at the moment, I keep seeing a dangerous party advancing on us."

The spy-glass passed from hand to hand, Jack and Ernest having run to their mother's perch agreed in thinking the moving objects were men on horseback. But when it was my turn to look, I was thrilled to be able to pronounce them to be very large ostriches.

"This is fortunate indeed!" I exclaimed. "If we can corral them by way of your brother's rope fence, we can release them onto the pirate party. They can be quite dangerous when agitated."

As the ostriches approached, we began to consider how we could attempt a capture. Fritz was much better at these things. But since I was relatively clearheaded for a sixty-year-old stoner, I ordered Ernest to recall the dogs, while Jack and I finished a corral of sorts by adding more string to one section of the valley. We draped it high and low so that the ambulating birds could not escape.

The ostriches continued to move in our direction, varying their pace as though in sport, springing, trotting, galloping, and chasing each other round and round, so that their approach was by no means rapid.

"I do not believe we have a chance with these birds," I said, "unless Ernest can send those dogs in pursuit. For that, we must bide our time and let them come as near as possible."

We held Turk and Juno concealed until the stately birds suddenly heard my thoughts—which had worried me—and began to appear uneasy.

Turk gave me one of his cryptic and menacing looks that normally meant he was about to take *us* over, but in this case, my mind was telling me his dominance was directed toward our enemy. Had this beast finally become our comrade? It would have brought a tear to my eye, but I was distracted as the beasts became impatient and furiously struggled from our grasp in an attempt to rush toward our astonished visitors. Once the birds were past us, we let them go. In an instant, the winged creatures fled with the speed of the wind—thanks to the dogs, they went in the right direction—their feet seemed not to touch the ground as they soared over land, their wings aiding their rapid progress.

In a few moments, they would be within our reach. Turk and Juno ushered the birds to exactly the spot we wished. Prepared, I finished off the hold with three loops of the rope, tightly attached to the final tree.

The voices of the ostriches were deep and hollow, a rumbling sound, much resembling the roar of the lion. We all felt that our new weapon would be a fearsome one indeed.

Meanwhile, Franz, who had returned to his perch, could be seen wildly waving his cap, and beckoning excitedly.

He ran a little way toward us, shouting: "It's them. I can see them! They are upon us! Move quickly!" We all hastened to our spots and, a short way off, beheld more than twenty men, making their way to Dankhurst.

CHAPTER 25

The Attack

I advanced with my loaded pistol to within a very few paces of the survivors and asked hesitantly, "So—do you guys party?"

When the danger was upon us, I saw Jack wave his arms in signal. The fire blazed from inside the first coconut as it was thrown onto the war party assembled below. As it exploded in the face of one of the pirates, weapons were raised to the ready throughout the crowd. They were a motley crew—long stringy hair covered in scarves and hats, skin leathery and worn. To see them at this distance filled me with a terrific dread. But now the bundles of blazing coconuts were dropping at a fast pace.

The action of the flames did little to ignite the dried brush throughout the valley. I scanned the perimeter and saw that the rope fence remained intact to keep the pirates from an easy retreat should they attempt to make one.

I saw that the actions of the boys had begun attracting the pirates' fire, although I wished a more efficacious remedy could have been had that did not involve putting my boys in the line of rockets and other gnarly ammo. As more pirates raised weapons, explosives flew into the trees, blowing several of them clean out of the ground and leaving radiant meteors of round and barren land lighted up and displayed as if by the wand of an evil sorcerer. My blood boiled as I watched them converge beneath my good boys and take aim at them.

I waited no longer, and I heartened a little when I saw that Jack and Ernest had again begun throwing down their lighted coconuts—I felt that now or never was the moment for attack!

Calling on my sons to maintain their courage and presence of mind, I swiftly opened the ostrich pen and watched the birds in confusion at first attempt to flee from battle; however, Turk and Juno, along with good old Mr. Nips, in all manner of noise and frenzy, approached them from behind with rapid steps to coerce them forward by force if not will.

The dogs dashed forward to join in the fray, pushing the feathered creatures toward the pirates. Although I tried to call the dogs back, they would not retreat. Nips, to my relief, I saw, had climbed a high bough of an old fig tree to watch matters unfold out of the line of fire.

This was the signal to the whole party to begin our attack in earnest. The enemy bellowed loudly and ran around using their weapons to tear apart anything they could. I saw them trying to dash toward the boys. I, too, was now at great risk as massive explosions blasted around me. I did not have time to step behind a rock before one of the pirates spotted me and began to run full speed in my direction. Meanwhile, Jenny freed the logs, which began to roll down the hill at such a rate that the gun I had reached for was knocked free from my hand and rendered useless as it met with one of the fat rolling shafts. As the great boles tumbled, the pirate fast approached, missing death under crushing weight by sheer luck. I managed to draw a second pistol and fire. I missed, but in terror he fell back.

The advance of the rest of the men was then brought to a stop by a thunderous rumble from atop the mountain. Down poured a great torrent of water. The men halted, turned tail, and made an attempt to gallop, along with the ostrich flock, off across the plain. They did not succeed but were instead felled by the flood. I managed to climb up a nearby rock to a higher altitude. The dogs still held gallantly to the attackers. They dragged and tussled with them, but with the rise of the water, they found they had to refocus their efforts on regaining their footing upon a high boulder.

I did not know how to assist the dogs and watched with relief as they scrambled to safety.

As the water receded, we saw that nearly half our attackers were immobilized. The ones still standing were overcoming the shock of our attack, many coughing and making all effort to catch their breath. Now the boys, Jenny, and Elizabeth met me where I was perched in preparation to defend Dankhurst.

The rustling of the birds gave way to crackling and creaking among the branches, with horrid cries, and shrieks, and chattering, all of which increased to a degree sufficient to make my hands and heart tremble. The whole disorderly rabble scrambled and sprung, racing and tumbling across the grass in every direction. The men grabbed their fallen comrades as they made their way to escape a battery of feet, feathers, and beaks.

From where we watched, the entire display seemed truly innumerable—and the confused, rapid way both man and bird swarmed here and there made it difficult to judge accurately how many remained. Some continued to dash about fearfully in all directions, others scrambled and did battle with ropes guarding the perimeter, until at last one broke through and our feathered allies, one and all, ran for the hills.

The panic being general, the two dogs, whose thirst for power over us had always been nearly uncontrollable, now rushed to attack the men, as though burning with zeal to execute justice upon desperate criminals.

The place soon had the appearance of a ghastly battle-field, and we were obliged to do our part to bat away the dogs with clubs and sticks until the din of howling, yelling, barking, in every conceivable tone of rage and pain gave way to an awful silence, and we looked with a shudder on the shocking spectacle around us.

With guns raised, my brave family and I advanced slowly to meet the survivors. Jack was ready to fire, but Ernest was such a mess of nerves that we encouraged him to bring up the rear. We fired together on the heap of pirates but not one bullet hit. We found it most difficult to take aim after this, as the dogs had begun to herd the pirates into a group.

At least fourteen pirates lay mangled and exhausted, while six stood trembling as they waited for the next assault.

Watching for our opportunity, I told my family to lower their weapons. I advanced with my loaded pistol to within a very few paces of the survivors and asked hesitantly, "So—do you guys party?"

The men looked at me blankly.

"Maybe they don't speak English," suggested Jack.

"I know they do," said Jenny. "I remember *that* one from when my grandfather and I were left here for dead." She resolutely spit on the ground in front of him. He had long matted hair tied up in a ponytail and was wearing a Ben & Jerry's Chubby Hubby T-shirt over his otherwise bulky frame.

"What do you want from us?" that one asked.

"What do you want from *us*?" I countered.

"Are you kidding?" he asked. "We want your island! This place is worth a fortune."

"It's *our* island!" cried Jenny.

"That's what he said," I pointed out.

"Wait, what?" Jenny paused, confused.

The man made a move for his gun, but when Ernest's gun went off behind us, everyone dropped their weapons and ran for cover.

"That one shouldn't have a gun," said the pirate. We all shrugged because he was right.

With the dogs doing most of the heavy work, we disarmed the pirates and led them back to Dankhurst. They passed looks of utter amazement from one to the other as we took them up our tree-trunk stairway to the lookout where we secured them and then blocked any possible way out.

"Thank Jah!" I cried, as we emerged from the house to await Fritz and Franz and discuss our victory and what to do with our prisoners. "We have escaped the greatest peril we have yet encountered!"

Now, all of us, giddy with our great success, danced together at the foot of our castle, the villains locked away in the tower. We ate smoked snake jerky and then, having done more than our share for the safety of our island and lifestyle, we skinned up and enjoyed the sunset.

"Where's Ernest?" Jenny asked as I opened my eyes to brightest sunlight.

Although it was unintentional, everyone had fallen asleep, and the sun had both set and risen again. We quickly ran for the tree-trunk staircase only to discover at the top that our prisoners were no longer imprisoned.

Looking down at the ground, I saw to my horror the noble Turk bloodied and killed. I ran down and picked up his large head in my hands, cradling it there, missing my arch-nemesis and true friend. Nearby, his Juno moaned inconsolably. But the worst was still to come. On a nearby tree, ominously hung with a knife forced into the bark was a note:

"Dearest family,

I have been taken by pirates. Love to all.

Ernest"

"Oh poor boy!" I cried. "How will we recover him?"

"I don't know," said his mother. "But we must find him—today." She sighed and fretted the scenes of danger into which her sons were now passing, declaring she would much rather have them safe home again, accepting Jenny's arms as the girl went to console her.

We followed the trail the pirates had cut through the dank weed. On approaching the greenhouses beyond the Alaskan ThunderFuck patches, we were startled to hear human laughter, repeated again and again. Juno growled and drew close to us, while Jack practically leaped in rage right into the rice swamp.

The laughter continued.

"Something is very wrong!" cried Jenny. "I don't know how we shall be able to advance cautiously to see what they are doing as long as this dog is in such a rage."

"I will wait here with Juno," said my wife. "You go get my son!"

The three of us pressed on while Elizabeth wrapped the dog's leash about her arm and sat down for leverage, so desperate was the animal for the revenge she sought for her beloved Turk.

We made our way among the bushes with our guns drawn, until, through an opening in the thicket, we could see at the distance of about forty paces an enormous fire and our son's captors in the most wonderful state of excitement. Ernest danced around and uttered nonsensically as the hysterical laughter of his abductors pealed through the forest.

The boy kept running backward and forward, rising on his heels, and then rapidly whirling round and round, nodding his head, and going through the most frantic and ludicrous antics.

Ready to spring out at them, we waited until, calming down, the hyenas' laughter subsided. At Jack's lead, we came out of our hiding place and into the clearing, guns drawn. One look at us, and the menacing troupe broke into peals of renewed laughter. A few mimicked our move, using their hands as weapons pretending to shoot and kill each other while attempting to keep in check their unbridled hysterics.

"Wait!" broke forth Ernest. "Don't shoot."

One by one we put down our guns. "Father, Jack, Jenny, I'd like you to meet Floss and Bruno," the English-speaking pirate from the day before wiped his eyes and did a full bow before us. Floss, on the other hand, we could now see, with her hat removed, was a lady—or at least a female person—dressed up in men's clothing. She seemed to have taken a special liking to Ernest.

"That is Hubert, that's Sonny, Jose, and McLovin' . . . that one's Brucey and that's Mike . . . ." We waited until the boy had run through the names of more than twenty men, and surprisingly several burly women, until finally he came to the last. "And this is Cat." Pulling a black hood from her head, a beautiful young girl of about sixteen made us all audibly gasp.

"How do you do?" she asked, shaking Jenny's hand politely.

"I gave them the Magic Kush!" exclaimed Ernest. "I had a bud of it in my pocket and they wanted to smoke it and we did and now . . . ."

The pirate Bruno high-fived my son. And with no prompting beyond that, we packed up another and got onboard the Magic Kush with the pirates.

CHAPTER 26

Pirate Captain Grizzle

*"A castle of marijuana.
Would you look at that?"*

At the end of the day, we agreed to make our way back to Dankhurst for the night with our guests. It was only now occurring to us that there had been no word from Fritz or Franz. Not wanting to think the worst, we confided in our new friends.

Unfortunately, our news was not met with much reassurance. Bruno explained that the pirate captain was a man named Grizzle. He was an angry man just as they had been before riding the Magic Kush. But, Bruno explained, Grizzle was not just angry, he was money hungry. He had been set upon returning to this island for the five years since he'd first set eyes on it. And if Grizzle had gotten his hands on Fritz and Franz, there would be no mercy. He planned to take this place by force.

Bruno did believe, however, that Grizzle was a complete moron, which is why it had taken them five years to find their way back. He suggested we make an attempt to appeal to Grizzle's vanity. If we treated him with all the honor of a decorated general, he might let us go. But first, we would need to be prepared to barter with him to get our boys back.

I formulated a plan and then set about its execution at daybreak. We assembled in our little kitchen at the base of the castle. A small meal was eaten hurriedly and almost in silence, for our hearts were too full and our minds too busily occupied to allow any outward display of anxiety. Ernest and Jack then slipped quietly out and presently returned from the garden with baskets of the choicest fruits in fresh and fragrant profusion, and with these as presents for the strangers, we boarded our boat, leaving behind the girls and our new friends—all except Bruno who insisted that he come along and attempt to smooth over the talks between the parties.

The anchor was weighed, the sails set, and we bounded across the waters of Safety Bay, giving a wide berth to the reef, against whose frowning rocks the sea still lashed itself. We made way for the cove, where the pirate ship awaited us.

Every eye onboard turned toward us when we came into view. Every glass was fixed upon our every motion. Because of all the strange sights on which the menacing crew might have looked, such an anomaly as a pleasure boat manned by a party such as us, and cruising upon this strange shore, was the furthest from their thoughts.

We pulled for the brig until in another minute we were upon her deck. Holding up a white hemp cloth as ordered by my wife, we watched the captain walk toward us with a heavy foot, compounded by a wooden leg, a heavy Scottish brogue, and a colorful parrot riding on one of his two broad shoulders that croaked, "Polly hates stoners." In silence we were led into his cabin and asked to explain what he owed God and the devil for this visit from a bunch of ugly hippies.

Not seeing Fritz or Franz anywhere, I gave the terrifying man a short history of our wreck, and our time upon these shores, and all the good we had done them.

"Then," said the sarcastic mate, rising and grasping my hand, "let me heartily thank you for I plan to relieve you of them at once."

He then squeezed my hand death grip–style until I was crippled under the pressure and bent nearly under the table around which we had convened.

"Where's Fritz?" asked Jack out of turn, taking some of the unwanted attention off me and hopefully not putting his brothers in any further peril at the same time.

"Fritz!" bellowed the man laughing. "That's a funny name."

"Look, *Grizzle*, these dudes just want to go back to tending the island," offered good old Bruno.

"Well," the captain said, plainly unmoved by the speech, "these *dudes*," he said like he was spitting, "can absolutely stay!" He smiled a broad smile and everyone breathed out ready to smile broadly back with relief, until he added, "They'll just have to pay a little rent to live on *Grizzland*."

I shuddered. How would we pay rent—in homemade Hot Pockets?

"Look," he went on, lowering his voice. "I'm a reasonable man. I will give you a fair deal: How about ten thousand a month, right, Seymour?" An old toothless pirate, likely named Seymour, laughed at his captain's terrible joke. "Ten thousand a month is a reasonable price for a nice private island. And since you are already moved in, I'll start with a security deposit, right now." The evil man looked horribly upon me. "So, will that be check or charge?"

With that, a din of laughter erupted around us. Carefully Ernest with his basket of fruit stepped forward and placed the cornucopia in front of Captain Grizzle. The gray beard lifted a whole unripened pineapple, outer armor and all, and bit straight through to the meat, ripping his own mouth bloody and following it up with a deep bone-chilling laugh.

"This," he said through blood and drool, "is neither check nor charge!"

"What can we do instead, Captain?" I asked. "For we have been out of civilization for so long, we have no money."

"Pay me in pirates," the old beast said in a raspy voice. With that, my young Franz and my brave Fritz were brought forth, standing, arms and feet shackled, with not a small deal of bruising about their faces. "Five thousand per boy. I'll take two to start. You can give me those two next month."

"You can't have my children!" I gasped.

"Then I'll have me my money."

"I will give you something of greater value than a few weak stoners," I said. "But it is on the island. You must come with me if you want to see it."

"What have you then?" Grizzle asked.

"I have a castle on the island and it is yours if you will give me back my children and let us leave here at once."

Fritz and Ernest gasped while my two youngest cried out, "No!"

"A castle, you say?" asked the old pirate. "I have six castles. Why do I need another?"

"This castle is special," I told him. "For it is made out of thousands of bricks of Big Bud marijuana. It is an amazing thing to behold, and if you'll give me my children back, we will show you to our home and give it over to you and your men."

"And if I don't?"

"You may kill us now, but know it is well camouflaged among the reefer. You might spend a lifetime searching for it."

After a moment's thought, the captain said, "A grass castle—hmm. Might make an excellent tourist attraction. I will prepare a boat for us!" His final words proved enough of an order to set up a frenzy of pirate activity.

"He will kill us," whispered Fritz. "Mark my words. The minute you show him Dankhurst he will kill us and keep our home."

I looked imploringly at Bruno who shrugged in agreement with the boy's assessment.

One of the pirates led me by my arm while others flanked each of my children. We were led into a small vessel, Bruno slipping in among them and keeping his head low.

As soon as we arrived onshore, I sent Bruno ahead to Dankhurst to order my wife to make up the palace in as comely a fashion as she could with only a few minutes' lead. I wanted lanterns aglow in every window and hung low across our fields. I wanted the carcass of poor Turk to be cleaned up. And most important, I wanted Jenny to fire up her ovens with her magic bread. I hoped that food might send excellent smells from all over the grounds to temp our intruders. My new friend vowed to do so and, as such, set off.

Back at the boat I had each boy in turn express a need to relieve himself, each at a separate interval so that my wife and Jenny might be able to complete the task to which

Bruno was going to set them. I caused a ruckus of my own when I pretended to fall over in a weakened state until Grizzle became suspicious and forced me onward.

When we arrived at the glorious Dankhurst, my heart soared when I saw that it was as I had hoped. Alight with beautiful colored lanterns just as the sun bid his nightly farewell. Excellent smells came pouring out of the kitchen including Jenny's delectable maniac-bread, just as I'd instructed. The pirates we had left there earlier that day flanked the yard feigning their everyday sinister scowls so as to keep quelled any suspicion of their captain. They were no longer his followers at heart.

Captain Grizzle stood in silence beneath the great structure. Then, suddenly he let out a monstrous laugh that silenced even our aviary.

"A castle of marijuana. Would you look at that?"

"Welcome to Dankhurst, Captain Grizzle," I said. "Now please sit as our guest and let us serve you."

Without hesitation the evil man agreed, ordering his pirate cronies hither and thither to watch over us and shoot on sight should we make any false move. Ernest, Jack, Elizabeth, and I toured the man through the kitchen area, up the back stairs to the two bedrooms, then up into Jenny's turret, stopping briefly in the commode room that had been recently fashioned by Fritz, which guided our waste, via India rubber–covered bamboo piping, straight into a deep well that finally took it downstream.

The great pompous man used it right in front of my wife who shielded her eyes in horror.

When we returned to the outside, Fritz sat pouting and staring off over the great fields he had spent so many hours tending, and then returning his gaze to the home he had built with his own two hands. I squeezed his shoulder with affection as I leaned down and told him, "This place matters not-at-all without all of us in it."

"But we could make a deal with Grizzle, Father," he insisted. "We could get him his rent, start a business with him. We could be rich!"

At this, I knelt before my good boy and taking his face in my hands, I said, "We are far richer without the likes of this Captain Grizzle than we could ever be *with* him. You are right, Fritz. This was our island—*Stonerland*. But it can only be ours if we can keep it to ourselves—*for* ourselves."

My son sighed heavily and turned away from me.

The pirates were now drinking our stores of wine and laughing wildly, shooting at the little birds aflutter in the trees. Then they laughed heartily as the poor creatures dropped to the ground with a thud. I went into the house to assist Jenny and Elizabeth as this terrible night wore on. Luckily, Jack and Ernest had gotten a doobie lit and managed to sneak it around to each of us for a momentary reprieve.

We fed the pirates six smoked hams, eight cauldrons of flamingo stew, and an assortment of Elizabeth's unparalleled Hot Pockets. Jenny served her maniac-bread as a side dish, which I saw Grizzle chomp up in large quantity. We gave him the last of our four-year-old Twinkies too, which were fresher than we'd expected after five years on this damp island so we ended up sharing a few ourselves. Then, unsure if it was the stress or the Twinkies, we all started hallucinating. At this point, I thought it the right time to invite our guest to stay over.

I brought Grizzle into one of the upstairs bedrooms and left him there. Then, rejoining my family, I told them the plan.

CHAPTER 27

Dankhurst in Flames

"I understand that there is a world out there . . . with Narcs and people who don't believe Jesus smoked tons of doobage. . . . What kind of a world is that?"

With Grizzle now asleep in the castle, all the other pirates were watching us vigilantly for any false move. Two particularly large men stationed themselves at either side of the door. Our party now consisted of my family, Jenny, Bruno, Floss, the sixteen or so additional pirates whose names I had forgotten, and young Cat, who, I noticed, had met Franz and was standing quite close to him.

We all agreed that Bruno and the other pirates should execute our objective since any uncharacteristic movement out of the rest of us might lead to an immediate gunshot to the head. Explaining where the Paraphernalia box sat in our stockroom, the pirates made way.

After fifteen or twenty minutes, they emerged in a noticeable cloud of smoke and did not meet our eyes. Then, as the minutes crept by, one by one, at an excruciating pace, we heard first a crack followed by another crack. And as the dry bricks of our castle met with the lighters and matches of our pirate friends, our castle slowly went up in smoke!

In the ensuing mayhem, I organized my family—who were momentarily frozen by the growing flames painting their faces in dancing light—to run as fast as they could. With Fritz and Jenny hand-in-hand leading the way, followed by Ernest who was quite fast when overcome by sheer terror, and then Jack and Elizabeth. I came up last, dragging my young Franz who had not wanted to leave his new and pretty friend. Nips, rounding out the group, held tight to Franz's shoulder.

We made our way through the Big Bud grove, over the bridge at Strawberry Fields Forever River until we reached the bay. Taking the pirates' craft around the rocky coast, we made our way toward the looming ship, ghostly with all its crew ashore. Once we were safely on deck and Fritz was running around trying to figure out how to launch it, the rest of us paused to watch the flames as they rose up from the dense forest of our island.

Tears ran down Jenny's cheeks freely, for what I believed were both the home we had lost and the relief at having fled our certain death. Franz, on the other hand, had welled up with great tears over a girl-pirate and the loss of his favorite bong.

Fritz, meanwhile, continued to frantically run from stern to stem until finally he called out for help. Jack ran to assist in pulling up the anchor when suddenly Jenny called out in a voice that did not sound like hers, "I don't trust this!"

Everyone stopped and looked at her.

"Trust what?" Fritz called out.

"You!" Jenny replied. "I can't believe you would go this far to take us from this place if you were not planning some-thing, Fritz Robinson!"

Halting his work, the boy approached his waiting family. "What do you mean? This was my father's idea. Get us off the island, away from these pirates."

"But he's paranoid and high. What's your excuse?" Jenny asked.

Fritz turned away in his rage, preparing to carry on with his work, but then suddenly he returned to the side of his love and offered, pleadingly, "We will leave the pirates here, trapped on the island. Then we will prepare to invade them sometime down the line. In that time we can set up contacts, make deals, get some capital to start up Fritz and Jenny Robinson Bud, LLC!"

Everyone stood back, listening in horror to the plan Fritz had just laid out.

"Fritz," Jenny said, taking his cheeks in her hands. "We don't need that!"

The boy continued to look at her with desperation in his eyes. "But you have to understand that . . . ."

"What, Fritz?" Jenny asked. "What do I have to understand? I understand that there is a world out there in which I do not want my child . . . *our* child to grow up! It is a world with Narcs and people who don't believe Jesus smoked tons of doobage. It is a skeptical place where people *don't* believe the Beatles sent the aliens complex messages recorded backward on at least six of their twenty-four albums! What kind of a world is that?"

Jenny paused while it sunk in finally that she was pregnant, which made us all happy.

"But what about Stallone movies and Sbarro Pizza?" Fritz asked.

Jenny took Fritz into a tight embrace and whispered, "We have it all right here!"

Just then Fritz pulled back and looked from his girl to his family and asked, "Then where are we going on this boat?"

Everyone shrugged as a few suggestions were bandied about.

"Humboldt? Amsterdam? The Olive Garden for bottomless breadsticks?"

At last we, the Robinsons, came to a collective agreement. Stonerland was *our* island and we would make a final attack on the pirates to take it back!

Having much experience rummaging around old ships, we split up to collect arms and other useful implements of attack. Fritz returned with a shield, a crossbow around his neck, along with an arrow backstop full of colorful feathered bows that distracted us momentarily as we each shared which color was our favorite.

Next Jack appeared, trumping his brother with a supercool electric *automatic* crossbow that sent Fritz into a real scowl. Jenny found an impressive fukimi-bari set she planned to use to take the pirates by surprise and then follow it up with a *pow-pow* of a really cool antique Weston. Jenny's gun was showed up by Franz's Uzi discovery and then overtaken by my wife's amazing pulse rifle find. Ernest brought up the rear with a battery-powered record player he intended to ask Fritz to make solar so that he might finally get to hear that Hendrix album we'd found.

I brought along Grizzle's four dogs as a peace offering to Juno whom we had only moments before planned to leave on the island with a bunch of pirates.

With that, we boarded the Robinson cruiser with our monkey and headed back toward the flames.

By the time we arrived back at Dankhurst, the worst of the fire had ceased to blaze. A few patchy brushfires remained. But for the most part, a thick dank smoke we were more used to having *in* our lungs then *out* hung heavily in the air. There was little noise, however, spreading outward from the source of the flames, but we strode on with as much care as we could. I kept the dogs quiet and close to my body lest they should try to run.

At last we emerged, weapons drawn, into the Big Bud clearing just as the sun began its ascent over the horizon. There, in the hazy morning light, stood the startling remains of our castle. We could not help but gasp in horror as this regal home had gone from green and vibrant to black and charred.

The place was unnaturally quiet. It was as if the pirates themselves had burned with Dankhurst.

Then, out of one patch of bushes came a high-pitched noise and a rustling. All five of my armed family members loaded and cocked their weapons, while Ernest hid behind his mother. I held tightly to the dogs but was ready at any moment to release and command them with my capable powers of ESP.

Suddenly, a body emerged, white in the morning light and as naked as the day the doctor had slapped his ass and called him Johnny. Jenny and Elizabeth covered their eyes in horror. The rest of us couldn't help but giggle as the man, without a second glance in our direction, ran past. Then we heard the gentle *thump thump thump* of a drum in the distance, followed by the *tap tap tap* of a cymbal. We made our way toward the sound, following a path haphazardly cut through the weeds. It led us straight to the beach, beyond which there was a glorious pastel-colored sunrise.

There all of the pirates had assembled, bringing with them all of the instruments passed out from the music equipment room. Leading the drum circle was our good friend Bruno and dancing around it was Cat, several other pirates, and, in the middle of it all, Captain Grizzle playing out a lovely verse of "Me and My Bobby McGee" on harmonica.

My family and I looked in on the beautiful scene. Dankhurst had burned and instead of lighting up our enemies, it had, quite plainly, lighted them up. Setting down our weapons, we continued to approach them with caution. Grizzle finished with the mouth harp and was swaying to the music.

"Ah!" he chortled noticing our arrival. "Yes! Join us!" He waved a large hand to beckon us closer.

Franz went first, rushing in to dance with the lovely Cat who encircled her arms around him happily and with a shy smile. Jack, pulled down onto the lap of a large bearded pirate, seemed to be in seventh heaven and I found that I was glad for him. Meanwhile, Ernest started Hendrix up on the portable record player to everyone's great joy.

Fritz and Jenny moved in time to the music, holding each other close. I saw my boy gingerly place a hand over the young lady's tiny stomach bump and kiss her cheek gently. Then I took my wife in my arms and danced with her as a great sun rose over Stonerland.

The music of Hendrix and our new pirate neighbors echoed around us, as we each sparked up a joint and smoked it.

EPILOGUE

Life on Stonerland resumed a comfortable normalcy.

We taught the pirates how to survive on our island, from bread baking to harvesting cannabis. We rebuilt Dankhurst with more turrets and more rooms than it ever had before, including a nursery. Other pot-houses were built for our new neighbors, and everyone pitched in to help build them, or at least Fritz did.

We learned more about our pirate friends, too. It turned out that Cat was Captain Grizzle's daughter. He had lost his wife to a series of robbery charges back in Milwaukee and, in despair, had decided to take up piracy. But ever since the night of the fire, he decided he just wanted to make music. After killing and eating his parrot for refusing to say anything but "Polly hates stoners," he became a vegetarian and gave up violence completely.

Nips grew old with us, remaining my children's life-long pet. Meanwhile, Juno never fully recovered from Turk's death but was mother to his puppies and shared them happily with all the citizens of the island.

Franz and Cat fell in love, and one day started a family of their own.

For a while Jack and the hairy pirate were an item but over time Gay Rules got in the way when they couldn't decide if they'd agreed to "No Last Names" or if it had just been a suggestion.

Meanwhile, Ernest became very good at fishing.

Jenny gave birth to a son and then restarted the Great Experiment at the letter E. However, halfway through to El Greco, she got pregnant with a little girl and then another girl, followed by twin boys. She was unable to complete the task before most of us had forgotten about it anyway and it had become more of an inside joke between her and Fritz. Fritz was the leader of the island. But mostly he just made sure we didn't forget to tend the fields so that the children would not one day be without a great and healthy harvest of bud. He also was the one who suggested we melt down the iron from all the weapons and make cool sculptures out of them.

And Elizabeth and I lived out our long lives on this great island in happiness watching our children and grandchildren thrive in freedom with an unending marijuana supply. There was only one unanswered question we all shared. Who had come before us and left us the greenhouses, hydroponic gardens, and acres of farmed land?

There were many suggested answers bandied about during all of our nights of splendid drug-induced speculation. But the greatest was this:

Long ago a family had been shipwrecked just off this very island. They had been on their way to begin a new colony when a storm hit their vessel. The resourceful group made their way with whatever supplies they could carry to this place and built a new life for themselves. Their name, it is said, was also Robinson.

But they weren't stoned, you see, they were Swiss—

The End

ABOUT THE AUTHORS

J. D. Wyss was a Swiss author who lived from 1743–1818, which disclaims in part the pointless gorilla massacre he invents in his masterpiece *The Swiss Family Robinson*. As a pastor and father, he wanted to write an adventure book like *Robinson Crusoe*, written by English author Daniel Defoe. Wyss's book, titled in Swedish *The Swiss Robinson* (for *Robinson Crusoe*), was released in 1812, and two years later released in English with its present title—which added "Family"—perhaps a typo, or maybe intentional (although Robinson is not a Swiss name). No member of the Wyss family was known in his lifetime as a stoner; however, one son was a musician—he wrote the Swiss national anthem. So that's cool.

J. P. Linder is an author and former stoner who still relishes the company of stoners and sparkly things. She has written several relationship guides, a few humor books, and even a book on the gamification of marketing. The biggest regret of her career is that in her book *The Purity Test* (St. Martin's Press, 2008), she failed to ask, "Have you ever taken a classic piece of valuable literature and bastardized it with obscenities and illegal drugs?" (Her answer is "Yes!") She lives with her future husband and their dog, Dee Dee Ramone (who does not look unlike her bass playing namesake). They live in Brooklyn and can never find a lighter.

DAILY BENDER

Want Some More?

Hit up our humor blog, The Daily Bender, to get your fill of all things funny—be it subversive, odd, offbeat, or just plain mean. The Bender editors are there to get you through the day and on your way to happy hour. Whether we're linking to the latest video that made us laugh or calling out (or bullshit on) whatever's happening, we've got what you need for a good laugh.

If you like our book, you'll love our blog. (And if you hated it, "man up" and tell us why.) Visit The Daily Bender for a shot of humor that'll serve you until the bartender can.

Sign up for our newsletter at
www.adamsmedia.com/blog/humor
and download our Top Ten Maxims No Man Should Live Without.